NATURAL GAS TRADING 101
Profit from the Energy Market

Usiere Uko

Copyright © 2024 Usiere Uko

All Rrghts reserved.

No part of this publication may be reproduced, distributed, or transmitted in any form or by any means, including photocopying, recording, or other electronic or mechanical methods, without the prior written permission of the publisher, except in the case of brief quotations embodied in critical reviews and certain other noncommercial uses permitted by copyright law.

This publication is designed to provide accurate and authoritative information in regard to the subject matter covered. It is sold with the understanding that the publisher is not engaged in rendering legal, accounting, or other professional services. If legal advice or other expert assistance is required, the services of a competent professional should be sought.

The author and publisher shall not be liable for any loss of profit or any other commercial damages, including but not limited to special, incidental, consequential, or other damages.

ISBN-13: 979-8-335-41909-3

FIRST EDITION

...To new frontiers, learning and growing

CONTENTS

Title Page
Copyright
Dedication
INTRODUCTION
PART 1: INTRODUCTION TO NATURAL GAS MARKETS   1
Chapter 1: Overview of Natural Gas as a Commodity   2
Chapter 2: Importance in the Global Energy Market   6
Chapter 3: Market Participants   11
Chapter 4: Key Concepts   17
PART 2: UNDERSTANDING THE NATURAL GAS SUPPLY CHAIN   24
Chapter 5: Exploration and Production   25
Chapter 6: Transportation and Storage   32
Chapter 7: Processing and Distribution   43
Chapter 8: The Role of Infrastructure in Market Dynamics   50
PART 3: NATURAL GAS PRICING AND MARKET STRUCTURES   58
Chapter 9: Understanding Spot and Futures Markets   59
Chapter 10: Pricing Hubs and Benchmarks   64
Chapter 11: Factors Influencing Natural Gas Prices   69
Chapter 12: Market Deregulation and Its Impact   75
PART 4: INTRODUCTION TO NATURAL GAS TRADING   80

INSTRUMENTS

Chapter 13: Spot Contracts … 81

Chapter 14: Futures Contracts … 87

Chapter 15: Options and Derivatives … 93

Chapter 16: Understanding CFDs … 100

PART 5: TECHNICAL ANALYSIS FOR NATURAL GAS TRADING … 106

Chapter 17: Chart Patterns and Trends … 107

Chapter 18: Moving Averages and Indicators … 114

Chapter 19: Volume Analysis … 125

Chapter 20: Using Technical Tools in Market Decision-Making … 132

PART 6: FUNDAMENTAL ANALYSIS FOR NATURAL GAS TRADING … 139

Chapter 21: Supply and Demand Factors … 140

Chapter 22: Economic Indicators and Their Impact … 147

Chapter 23: Weather Patterns and Seasonal Influences … 154

Chapter 24: Geopolitical Events and Their Effects on Prices … 162

PART 7: DEVELOPING A TRADING STRATEGY … 168

Chapter 25: Risk Management and Position Sizing … 169

Chapter 26: Combining Technical and Fundamental Analysis … 176

Chapter 27: Backtesting Your Strategy … 183

Chapter 28: Building a Trading Plan … 187

PART 8: RISK MANAGEMENT IN NATURAL GAS TRADING … 196

Chapter 29: Identifying and Mitigating Risks … 197

Chapter 30: Understanding Leverage and Margin … 203

Chapter 31: The Importance of Stop-Loss Orders	208
Chapter 32: Diversification Strategies	216
PART 9: TOOLS AND PLATFORMS FOR NATURAL GAS TRADING	223
Chapter 33: Selecting a Trading Platform	224
Chapter 34: Using Trading Software and Tools	235
Chapter 35: Accessing Market Data and Analysis Tools	243
Chapter 36: Choosing the Right Broker	253
PART 10: PRACTICAL CONSIDERATIONS	263
Chapter 37: Successful Natural Gas Trades	264
Chapter 38: Analyzing Market Trends and Historical Data	273
Chapter 39: Common Pitfalls and How to Avoid Them	279
PART 11: CONCLUSION AND NEXT STEPS	286
Chapter 40: Continued Learning Resources	287
Chapter 41: Final Tips for New Traders	292
About The Author	297
Books In This Series	299
Books By This Author	301

INTRODUCTION

A BEGINNER'S GUIDE TO PROFITING FROM THE ENERGY MARKET

The world of energy trading is vast, complex, and, for those who understand it, incredibly rewarding. At the heart of this dynamic market lies natural gas—a critical resource that powers industries, heats homes, and drives economies across the globe. As the demand for energy continues to grow and evolve, so too do the opportunities for traders who can navigate the intricacies of the natural gas market.

Welcome to ***Natural Gas Trading 101: A Beginner's Guide to Profiting from the Energy Market.*** Whether you're an aspiring trader, an energy enthusiast, or someone simply curious about the mechanics behind one of the world's most essential commodities, this book is designed to provide you with a solid foundation in natural gas trading.

WHY NATURAL GAS?

Natural gas is often referred to as a "bridge fuel"—a cleaner alternative to coal and oil that plays a crucial role in the transition toward a more sustainable energy future. But beyond its environmental benefits, natural gas is a highly traded commodity with significant profit potential for those who understand its market dynamics.

From the complexities of supply and demand to the influence of geopolitical events and weather patterns, the natural gas market is influenced by a myriad of factors. This volatility creates both challenges and opportunities for traders, making it an exciting and potentially lucrative field.

WHAT YOU'LL LEARN

This book is structured to guide you step-by-step through the world of natural gas trading. We begin with the basics—understanding what natural gas is, how it is produced, and how it reaches consumers. From there, we'll explore the various market structures, trading instruments, and analytical tools that are essential for making informed trading decisions.

You'll learn about the different strategies traders use to profit from price movements, how to manage risk effectively, and how to develop your own trading plan. Along the way, we'll also delve into real-world case studies and practical examples that illustrate key concepts and lessons.

WHO THIS BOOK IS FOR

Natural Gas Trading 101 is written for beginners who are new to the world of trading but are eager to learn. You don't need a background in finance or energy to benefit from this book—just a willingness to learn and a keen interest in the markets. By the end of this journey, you'll have the knowledge and confidence to begin trading natural gas and potentially profit from one of the most dynamic sectors of the global economy.

THE ROAD AHEAD

The energy markets are constantly evolving, driven by technological advancements, shifting regulations, and changing consumer behaviors. As you embark on this journey into natural gas trading, keep in mind that learning is a continuous process. This book will provide you with the tools and insights to get started, but the real mastery comes from experience and staying informed about the latest market developments.

So, whether you're looking to diversify your investment portfolio, start a new career in trading, or simply understand more about the energy markets, you're in the right place. Let's begin this exciting journey into the world of natural gas trading together.

Welcome to *Natural Gas Trading 101*.

PART 1: INTRODUCTION TO NATURAL GAS MARKETS

CHAPTER 1: OVERVIEW OF NATURAL GAS AS A COMMODITY

Natural gas is more than just a source of energy; it's a cornerstone of modern life, powering everything from industrial operations to residential heating. As a commodity, natural gas plays a crucial role in global markets, influencing economies, industries, and the environment. In this chapter, we will explore what natural gas is, how it fits into the broader energy landscape, and why it has become such an important commodity for traders and investors alike.

WHAT IS NATURAL GAS?

Natural gas is a fossil fuel formed over millions of years from the remains of ancient marine organisms. Composed primarily of methane (CH_4), it is found deep beneath the Earth's surface, often alongside oil deposits. Natural gas is extracted through drilling and is then processed and transported to consumers.

What sets natural gas apart from other fossil fuels is its relatively clean-burning nature. When combusted, natural gas emits fewer pollutants and greenhouse gases than coal or oil, making it a preferred choice for power generation and heating.

THE ROLE OF NATURAL GAS IN THE GLOBAL ENERGY MARKET

Natural gas is one of the most important energy sources in the world, second only to oil. Its versatility and abundance have made it a key player in the global energy market. Here's how natural gas is used across different sectors:

Electricity Generation: Natural gas is a major fuel for power plants, providing a reliable and flexible source of electricity. Its ability to quickly ramp up production makes it ideal for balancing supply with fluctuating demand.

Industrial Use: Many industries, such as chemicals, fertilizers, and manufacturing, rely on natural gas as both a fuel and a feedstock. It is used to produce heat, electricity, and various industrial products.

Residential and Commercial Heating: Natural gas is widely used for heating homes and buildings, as well as for cooking and water heating. Its efficiency and affordability make it a popular choice for residential and commercial consumers.

Transportation: Although less common, natural gas is also used as a fuel for vehicles, particularly in the form of compressed natural gas (CNG) or liquefied natural gas (LNG).

NATURAL GAS AS A TRADED COMMODITY

Natural gas is traded on global markets like any other commodity, such as oil, gold, or wheat. Its price is influenced by a variety of factors, including supply and demand dynamics, geopolitical events, weather patterns, and technological advancements.

The trading of natural gas typically occurs in two main forms: physical and financial.

Physical Trading: This involves the actual buying and selling of natural gas for delivery at a specific time and location. Physical traders are often involved in the production, transportation, or consumption of natural gas.

Financial Trading: This involves trading contracts that derive their value from the price of natural gas without the physical exchange of the commodity. Financial instruments such as futures, options, and contracts for difference (CFDs) allow traders to speculate on price movements or hedge against risks.

KEY NATURAL GAS MARKETS AND PRICING HUBS

The natural gas market is global but fragmented, with different pricing mechanisms in various regions. The most significant natural gas markets and pricing hubs include:

Henry Hub (United States): Located in Louisiana, Henry Hub is the primary pricing point for natural gas in North America. The prices here are widely used as a benchmark for U.S. natural gas.

National Balancing Point (NBP, United Kingdom): NBP is a virtual trading point for natural gas in the UK and serves as a major pricing hub for European markets.

Title Transfer Facility (TTF, Netherlands): TTF is another key European hub, providing a liquid market for natural gas trading across Europe.

Japan-Korea Marker (JKM): JKM is the benchmark price for LNG in Northeast Asia, reflecting the growing importance of liquefied natural gas in global trade.

Natural gas is a vital commodity with a significant impact on the global economy and energy landscape. Understanding its role, market dynamics, and pricing mechanisms is essential for anyone interested in trading or investing in this market. As we move forward in this book, we will delve deeper into the various aspects of natural gas trading, equipping you with the knowledge and tools to navigate this exciting and ever-evolving market.

CHAPTER 2: IMPORTANCE IN THE GLOBAL ENERGY MARKET

Natural gas holds a unique and increasingly critical position in the global energy market. Its role as a versatile, efficient, and relatively cleaner source of energy has made it indispensable in meeting the world's growing energy demands. In this chapter, we will explore the importance of natural gas within the global energy landscape, its impact on economies, its role in energy security, and its contribution to the ongoing energy transition.

THE ROLE OF NATURAL GAS IN GLOBAL ENERGY SUPPLY

Natural gas is one of the three primary fossil fuels, alongside oil and coal, that power the global economy. Its share in the global energy mix has been steadily increasing, driven by its wide range of applications across various sectors.

Electricity Generation: Natural gas is a key fuel for power generation worldwide. Its flexibility and efficiency make it an ideal choice for both base-load power plants and peaking plants, which are used to meet sudden spikes in electricity demand. Unlike coal, natural gas plants can be quickly ramped up or down, providing grid stability and supporting the integration of intermittent renewable energy sources like wind and solar.

Industrial Applications: The industrial sector is one of the largest consumers of natural gas. It is used not only as a fuel for heating and power but also as a feedstock in the production of chemicals, fertilizers, plastics, and other industrial products. Natural gas's high energy content and relatively low cost make it a preferred choice for industries seeking to optimize production and reduce emissions.

Residential and Commercial Use: Natural gas is widely used in homes and businesses for heating, cooking, and water heating. Its efficiency, affordability, and cleanliness have made it a staple in many households and commercial establishments, particularly in regions with well-developed natural gas infrastructure.

Transportation: While still a niche market, the use of natural gas as a transportation fuel is growing. Compressed natural gas (CNG) and liquefied natural gas (LNG) are increasingly used in vehicles, particularly in fleets and heavy-duty trucks, as a cleaner alternative to diesel and gasoline.

ECONOMIC IMPACT OF NATURAL GAS

Natural gas plays a significant role in the global economy, influencing everything from energy prices to trade balances. The economic impact of natural gas can be seen in several key areas:

Energy Prices: Natural gas prices are a major determinant of electricity and heating costs, which in turn affect industrial production, consumer spending, and overall economic growth. Regions with abundant and cheap natural gas resources, such as North America, have a competitive advantage in energy-intensive industries.

Job Creation and Investment: The natural gas industry supports millions of jobs worldwide, from exploration and production to transportation, distribution, and retail. It also attracts substantial investment in infrastructure, such as pipelines, storage facilities, and LNG terminals, which are critical for the efficient delivery of natural gas to markets.

Trade and Geopolitics: Natural gas is a major commodity in international trade, particularly in the form of LNG. Countries with large natural gas reserves, such as Russia, Qatar, and the United States, wield significant geopolitical influence as major exporters. Conversely, import-dependent countries often seek to diversify their supply sources to enhance energy security.

ENERGY SECURITY AND GEOPOLITICS

Energy security—ensuring a reliable, affordable, and sustainable supply of energy—is a critical concern for nations around the world. Natural gas plays a central role in energy security due to its importance in electricity generation and heating.

Supply Diversity: Countries that rely heavily on natural gas imports are vulnerable to supply disruptions, whether due to geopolitical tensions, natural disasters, or technical issues. As a result, many nations seek to diversify their supply sources by developing domestic resources, investing in LNG import infrastructure, or entering into long-term supply agreements.

Geopolitical Leverage: Natural gas exporters, particularly those with large reserves and infrastructure, can exert significant geopolitical influence. For example, Russia's dominance in European natural gas supplies gives it considerable leverage in regional politics. Similarly, the United States' emergence as a major LNG exporter has reshaped global gas markets and enhanced its geopolitical standing.

Pipeline Diplomacy: The construction and operation of natural gas pipelines often involve complex negotiations between countries, with significant geopolitical implications. Pipeline routes can determine market access, influence regional stability, and shape alliances.

NATURAL GAS AND THE ENERGY TRANSITION

The global push toward cleaner, more sustainable energy sources has placed natural gas at the center of the energy transition. While still a fossil fuel, natural gas is seen as a "bridge fuel" that can help reduce carbon emissions while renewable energy capacity is being built up.

Lower Carbon Emissions: Natural gas burns more cleanly than coal or oil, producing significantly lower levels of carbon dioxide (CO_2), sulfur dioxide (SO_2), and particulate matter. This makes it an attractive option for reducing emissions from power generation and industrial processes.

Complementing Renewables: Natural gas-fired power plants are highly flexible and can be quickly ramped up or down to complement intermittent renewable energy sources like wind and solar. This ability to provide reliable backup power is essential for maintaining grid stability as the share of renewables in the energy mix increases.

Challenges and Controversies: Despite its benefits, natural gas is not without its challenges. Methane, the primary component of natural gas, is a potent greenhouse gas that can leak during production, transportation, and storage. There is also ongoing debate about the long-term role of natural gas in a decarbonized energy system, with some advocating for a rapid phase-out in favor of renewables and others seeing it as a necessary component of the transition.

THE FUTURE OF NATURAL GAS IN THE GLOBAL ENERGY MARKET

The future of natural gas in the global energy market will be shaped by a variety of factors, including technological advancements, regulatory changes, market dynamics, and environmental considerations.

Technological Innovations: Advances in drilling techniques, such as hydraulic fracturing and horizontal drilling, have unlocked vast new reserves of natural gas, particularly in the United States. Innovations in LNG technology have also expanded the global reach of natural gas, enabling it to be transported over long distances and reaching markets that lack pipeline infrastructure.

Regulatory and Environmental Policies: Government policies on climate change, emissions reduction, and energy efficiency will play a major role in determining the future demand for natural gas. Stricter environmental regulations could accelerate the shift away from fossil fuels, while policies that promote natural gas as a cleaner alternative to coal could support its continued growth.

Market Dynamics: The global natural gas market is becoming increasingly interconnected, with LNG serving as a key link between regional markets. As more countries invest in LNG infrastructure, the global natural gas market is expected to become more liquid and competitive, with prices reflecting a wider range of factors.

Natural gas is a vital component of the global energy market, with significant economic, geopolitical, and environmental implications. Its role in electricity generation, industrial production, and residential heating, combined with its relative cleanliness and flexibility, make it a key player in the global energy landscape.

As the world continues to navigate the challenges of the energy transition, natural gas will remain an important, though sometimes controversial, part of the solution. Understanding its significance and the factors that influence its market is essential for anyone involved in or interested in energy trading.

CHAPTER 3: MARKET PARTICIPANTS

PRODUCERS, CONSUMERS, AND TRADERS

The natural gas market is a dynamic ecosystem that involves a wide range of participants, each playing a crucial role in the supply chain. Understanding these market participants—producers, consumers, and traders—is essential for anyone looking to navigate the complexities of natural gas trading. In this chapter, we will explore the roles and motivations of each group, their interactions within the market, and how they influence the overall dynamics of natural gas prices and availability.

PRODUCERS: THE SUPPLY SIDE OF THE MARKET

Producers are at the forefront of the natural gas market, responsible for extracting and supplying this vital resource. Their operations include exploration, drilling, extraction, processing, and in some cases, transportation of natural gas. Here's a closer look at the different types of producers and their roles:

Upstream Companies: These companies are involved in the exploration and production (E&P) of natural gas. They locate natural gas reserves, drill wells, and extract the gas from the earth. Major upstream companies include large multinational corporations like ExxonMobil, Chevron, and BP, as well as smaller independent firms that specialize in specific regions or types of natural gas resources.

Midstream Companies: After natural gas is extracted, it must be transported and processed before reaching consumers. Midstream companies are responsible for gathering, processing, transporting, and storing natural gas. They operate pipelines, storage facilities, and processing plants that clean the gas and prepare it for delivery to end users.

Liquefied Natural Gas (LNG) Producers: LNG producers are a specialized subset of natural gas producers who liquefy natural gas for transport across long distances, particularly to markets that are not accessible by pipelines. LNG production involves cooling natural gas to a liquid state, making it easier to transport via specialized tankers.

National Oil and Gas Companies (NOCs): In many countries, natural gas production is dominated by state-owned enterprises known as NOCs. These companies, such as Gazprom in Russia, Saudi Aramco in Saudi Arabia, and Petrobras in Brazil, play a significant role in global natural gas supply and often have substantial influence over national energy policies.

CONSUMERS: THE DEMAND SIDE OF THE MARKET

Consumers of natural gas are the end users who purchase and utilize natural gas for various purposes. The demand side of the market is diverse, encompassing a wide range of industries, residential users, and power generators. The main categories of natural gas consumers include:

Power Generation Companies: One of the largest consumers of natural gas is the power generation sector. Natural gas-fired power plants use gas to produce electricity, offering a cleaner alternative to coal and oil. These companies require a steady and reliable supply of natural gas to meet electricity demand, especially during peak periods.

Industrial Users: Industries such as chemicals, fertilizers, glass, steel, and cement rely heavily on natural gas as both a fuel and a raw material. Natural gas is used in industrial processes for heating, electricity generation, and as a feedstock for producing chemicals like ammonia and methanol. Industrial demand is often linked to economic activity, with higher demand during periods of economic growth.

Residential and Commercial Consumers: Homes and businesses use natural gas for heating, cooking, and hot water. In many regions, natural gas is the primary source of heating fuel due to its efficiency and affordability. Commercial consumers, such as office buildings, schools, and hospitals, also use natural gas for similar purposes.

Transportation Sector: Although still a relatively small portion of overall demand, the use of natural gas in transportation is growing. Natural gas vehicles (NGVs) powered by compressed natural gas (CNG) or liquefied natural gas (LNG) are becoming more common, particularly in fleets and public transportation systems.

Export Markets: Some countries export natural gas to other nations, either via pipelines or as LNG. Exporters rely on foreign demand to sell their surplus natural gas, and international trade plays a significant role in balancing supply and demand on a global scale.

TRADERS: THE INTERMEDIARIES OF THE MARKET

Traders are the intermediaries who buy and sell natural gas in the market, aiming to profit from price fluctuations. They play a crucial role in providing liquidity, managing risk, and ensuring that natural gas is delivered from producers to consumers efficiently. The main types of traders include:

Physical Traders: These traders are involved in the actual buying and selling of physical natural gas. They purchase gas from producers and sell it to consumers, such as utilities, industrial users, and power generators. Physical traders manage logistics, including transportation and storage, to ensure that natural gas is delivered where and when it is needed. Companies like Vitol, Glencore, and Trafigura are major players in physical trading.

Financial Traders: Financial traders do not take physical possession of natural gas but instead trade financial contracts based on the commodity. These contracts include futures, options, and swaps, which are used to speculate on price movements or hedge against risk. Financial traders include hedge funds, investment banks, and proprietary trading firms that operate in the natural gas futures markets, such as those on the New York Mercantile Exchange (NYMEX).

Speculators: Speculators are a type of financial trader who seek to profit from short-term price movements in the natural gas market. They take on significant risk in the hope of achieving high returns, often using leverage to amplify their positions. Speculators play a key role in providing liquidity to the market, but their activities can also contribute to increased volatility.

Hedgers: Hedgers use natural gas contracts to manage risk associated with price fluctuations. Producers, for example, may sell futures contracts to lock in prices for their gas, ensuring revenue stability even if market prices decline. Similarly, consumers, such as power plants, may purchase futures contracts to secure a fixed price for their gas supply, protecting themselves from potential price increases.

Market Makers: Market makers are financial firms that provide liquidity by continuously quoting buy and sell prices for natural gas contracts. Their activities help narrow bid-ask spreads, making it easier for other traders to enter and exit positions. Market makers earn a profit from the difference between the prices at which they buy and sell contracts.

THE INTERPLAY BETWEEN MARKET PARTICIPANTS

The natural gas market functions through the continuous interaction between producers, consumers, and traders. These interactions create a complex web of relationships that influence supply, demand, and prices. Understanding the interplay between these participants is crucial for anyone involved in natural gas trading.

Supply and Demand Dynamics: Producers respond to price signals by adjusting their output, while consumers adjust their consumption based on availability and cost. Traders, in turn, facilitate the movement of natural gas from regions of surplus to regions of demand, helping to balance the market. Changes in any of these factors can lead to price fluctuations, creating opportunities and risks for traders.

Price Discovery: Traders play a key role in price discovery—the process by which the market determines the price of natural gas. Through their buying and selling activities, traders aggregate information about supply and demand, geopolitical events, weather conditions, and other factors, which is reflected in market prices. This price discovery process is essential for efficient market functioning and informed decision-making by all participants.

Risk Management: Each group of market participants has its own set of risks, whether it's the price volatility faced by producers, the supply risks faced by consumers, or the market risks faced by traders. Risk management strategies, including hedging with financial instruments, are employed to mitigate these risks and ensure market stability.

The natural gas market is a complex and interconnected system involving a diverse range of participants, each with its own motivations and roles. Producers extract and supply natural gas, consumers drive demand, and traders act as intermediaries, ensuring the efficient flow of the commodity through the market. Understanding the roles of these participants and their interactions is key to navigating the natural gas market, whether you're a trader looking to capitalize on price movements or an investor seeking to understand the broader market dynamics.

CHAPTER 4: KEY CONCEPTS
SUPPLY, DEMAND, AND PRICE DYNAMICS

Understanding the key concepts of supply, demand, and price dynamics is essential for anyone looking to succeed in the natural gas market. These fundamental economic principles govern how natural gas is produced, consumed, and traded, and they have a direct impact on market prices. In this chapter, we will explore these concepts in detail, examining how they interact to shape the natural gas market and influence trading decisions.

SUPPLY DYNAMICS

Supply dynamics in the natural gas market refer to the various factors that affect the availability of natural gas. These factors include production levels, storage capacities, technological advancements, and geopolitical influences. Let's take a closer look at each of these elements:

Production Levels: The amount of natural gas produced is the primary driver of supply. Production levels are influenced by the availability of natural gas reserves, the cost of extraction, and the decisions made by producers based on market conditions. High production levels typically lead to an increase in supply, which can put downward pressure on prices. Conversely, low production levels can create supply shortages, driving prices up.

Storage: Natural gas is often stored in underground facilities, such as depleted oil and gas fields, salt caverns, or aquifers. Storage plays a crucial role in balancing supply and demand, particularly in regions with seasonal variations in consumption. During periods of low demand, excess natural gas is stored, and during periods of high demand, stored gas is withdrawn to supplement supply. Storage levels can have a significant impact on market prices, especially in anticipation of winter heating demand or summer cooling needs.

Technological Advancements: Innovations in drilling and extraction technologies, such as hydraulic fracturing (fracking) and horizontal drilling, have dramatically increased the supply of natural gas, particularly in regions like the United States. These advancements have unlocked vast reserves of shale gas, leading to a surge in production and a transformation of global natural gas markets.

Geopolitical Factors: The supply of natural gas is often influenced by geopolitical events, such as conflicts, trade disputes, or sanctions. For example, disruptions in supply from major producing regions, like the Middle East or Russia, can lead to sudden shortages and price spikes. Geopolitical tensions can also impact the development of new natural gas projects or the operation of existing infrastructure, further influencing supply.

DEMAND DYNAMICS

Demand dynamics refer to the various factors that affect the consumption of natural gas. These factors include economic growth, weather conditions, energy policies, and competition from other energy sources. Let's explore these elements in more detail:

Economic Growth: The demand for natural gas is closely linked to economic activity. During periods of economic expansion, industries ramp up production, leading to increased demand for natural gas as a fuel and feedstock. Similarly, higher levels of consumer spending can boost demand for electricity and heating, both of which rely on natural gas. Conversely, during economic downturns, demand for natural gas tends to decline as industrial activity slows and consumers cut back on energy use.

Weather Conditions: Weather is one of the most significant short-term drivers of natural gas demand. Cold winters and hot summers can lead to spikes in demand for heating and cooling, respectively. In winter, residential and commercial consumers rely on natural gas for heating, while in summer, natural gas-fired power plants often ramp up production to meet increased electricity demand for air conditioning. Unexpected weather events, such as polar vortexes or heatwaves, can cause sharp changes in demand and lead to volatile price movements.

Energy Policies: Government policies on energy use, emissions, and climate change can have a profound impact on natural gas demand. Policies that promote the use of cleaner energy sources, such as natural gas, over coal or oil can boost demand. Conversely, policies that encourage the adoption of renewable energy or impose restrictions on fossil fuel use can reduce demand for natural gas. Subsidies, taxes, and regulations all play a role in shaping the demand landscape.

Competition from Other Energy Sources: Natural gas competes with other energy sources, such as coal, oil, and renewables, for market share. The relative prices of these energy sources can influence demand for natural gas. For example, if coal prices fall significantly, power generators might switch from natural gas to coal, reducing demand for gas. Similarly, the growing competitiveness of wind, solar, and battery storage technologies could reduce reliance on natural gas for electricity generation in the long term.

PRICE DYNAMICS

Price dynamics in the natural gas market are the result of the interplay between supply and demand. Prices are constantly fluctuating in response to changes in market conditions, and understanding these fluctuations is key to successful trading. Here's how supply and demand interact to influence prices:

Equilibrium Price: The price of natural gas in a free market is determined by the point at which supply meets demand, known as the equilibrium price. At this price, the quantity of natural gas that producers are willing to supply matches the quantity that consumers are willing to purchase. If supply exceeds demand, prices tend to fall until equilibrium is restored. Conversely, if demand exceeds supply, prices rise until the market reaches a new equilibrium.

Price Volatility: Natural gas prices are known for their volatility, often swinging dramatically in response to changes in supply, demand, or external factors. Volatility can be driven by seasonal demand fluctuations, unexpected weather events, geopolitical tensions, or changes in production levels. Traders often seek to profit from this volatility by buying low and selling high, but it also presents risks, particularly for those who are unhedged.

Price Correlations: Natural gas prices are often correlated with the prices of other commodities, particularly oil and electricity. For example, in regions where natural gas competes directly with oil for power generation or heating, changes in oil prices can influence natural gas prices. Similarly, in markets where natural gas is a major fuel for electricity generation, natural gas prices may be correlated with electricity prices.

Market Sentiment: Trader sentiment, driven by news, reports, and market expectations, can also influence natural gas prices. Positive news about increased production, mild weather forecasts, or reduced geopolitical risks can lead to lower prices, while negative news, such as supply disruptions or extreme weather forecasts, can push prices higher. Market sentiment often leads to short-term price movements that may not be directly related to fundamental supply and demand factors.

THE ROLE OF STORAGE IN PRICE DYNAMICS

Storage plays a crucial role in balancing supply and demand and, by extension, in price dynamics. The ability to store natural gas allows market participants to manage fluctuations in supply and demand more effectively. Here's how storage impacts prices:

Seasonal Price Patterns: Storage levels typically rise during the warmer months when demand is lower, and fall during the colder months when demand peaks. This seasonal pattern often leads to predictable price fluctuations, with prices generally lower during the summer when storage is being filled, and higher during the winter when storage is being drawn down. Traders often use these seasonal patterns to inform their trading strategies.

Price Spikes and Dips: Storage can mitigate the impact of short-term supply disruptions or demand surges, preventing extreme price spikes or dips. For example, if a sudden cold snap leads to a spike in demand, stored gas can be withdrawn to meet the increased need, preventing prices from soaring. Conversely, if there is an unexpected drop in demand, producers might reduce output or store excess gas, preventing prices from collapsing.

Market Signals: Storage levels are closely monitored by market participants as an indicator of future price movements. High storage levels heading into winter, for example, might signal that prices are likely to remain stable or decline, while low storage levels could indicate the potential for price spikes if demand surges. Weekly storage reports, such as those released by the U.S. Energy Information Administration (EIA), are key market indicators that traders watch closely.

EXTERNAL FACTORS INFLUENCING SUPPLY, DEMAND, AND PRICES

In addition to the core supply and demand dynamics, several external factors can influence natural gas prices:

Weather Forecasts: Weather forecasts are one of the most important external factors influencing natural gas prices, particularly in the short term. Forecasts of colder-than-normal winters or hotter-than-normal summers can lead to anticipatory price movements as traders position themselves for expected changes in demand.

Geopolitical Events: Political instability, conflicts, trade disputes, and sanctions in key producing or consuming regions can lead to supply disruptions or changes in demand, impacting prices. For example, tensions in the Middle East or Eastern Europe, both of which are significant natural gas-producing regions, can lead to fears of supply shortages and price spikes.

Technological Developments: Advances in energy technology, such as improvements in renewable energy or battery storage, can influence long-term demand for natural gas. Conversely, breakthroughs in natural gas extraction or transportation technology can increase supply, potentially leading to lower prices.

Economic Indicators: Broader economic indicators, such as GDP growth, industrial output, and consumer spending, can influence natural gas demand. Strong economic growth typically leads to higher energy consumption, while a slowing economy may reduce demand for natural gas.

Supply, demand, and price dynamics are the fundamental forces that shape the natural gas market. By understanding how these forces interact, traders and investors can make more informed decisions and better anticipate market movements. Whether you are trading natural gas futures, investing in energy stocks, or simply looking to understand the market better, a solid grasp of these concepts is essential.

PART 2: UNDERSTANDING THE NATURAL GAS SUPPLY CHAIN

CHAPTER 5: EXPLORATION AND PRODUCTION

Exploration and production (E&P) form the backbone of the natural gas industry, encompassing the processes and technologies involved in locating, extracting, and preparing natural gas for sale and use. This chapter delves into the intricate stages of E&P, the key players involved, and the challenges and opportunities they face in bringing natural gas from the reservoir to the market.

THE EXPLORATION PHASE

Exploration is the first step in the natural gas production process. It involves identifying potential natural gas reserves, evaluating their viability, and determining the best locations for drilling. The exploration phase includes several critical steps:

1. GEOLOGICAL SURVEYS AND ANALYSIS

Geological surveys are used to identify areas that are likely to contain natural gas deposits. Geologists analyze the earth's structure, looking for specific rock formations, fault lines, and other indicators of natural gas presence. This analysis often involves:

Seismic Surveys: Seismic surveys are a primary tool for exploring natural gas reserves. These surveys use sound waves to create a map of the subsurface geology. By analyzing the way sound waves reflect off different geological layers, geologists can identify potential natural gas reservoirs.

Magnetic and Gravity Surveys: These surveys measure variations in the earth's magnetic and gravitational fields to detect subsurface structures that may indicate the presence of natural gas.

Geochemical Surveys: Geochemical surveys involve analyzing soil and water samples for traces of hydrocarbons, which can signal the presence of natural gas.

2. DRILLING AND TESTING

Once a potential site is identified, exploratory drilling begins. This process involves drilling a well to reach the target rock formation and extracting samples to determine the presence and quantity of natural gas. Key steps in this process include:

Wildcat Wells: These are the first wells drilled in a new area, intended to confirm the presence of natural gas. Wildcat wells are high-risk ventures, as there is no guarantee of success.

Appraisal Wells: If a wildcat well discovers natural gas, appraisal wells are drilled to assess the size and quality of the reservoir. These wells help determine the commercial viability of the site.

Flow Testing: Once a well is drilled, it undergoes flow testing to measure the rate at which natural gas can be extracted. This testing provides crucial data for determining the production potential of the reservoir.

3. RISK ASSESSMENT AND DECISION MAKING

Exploration is a high-risk, high-reward endeavor. Companies must weigh the potential for significant discoveries against the costs and risks of exploration. Factors considered in this decision-making process include:

Geological Risk: The uncertainty associated with the presence and size of natural gas reserves.

Technical Risk: The challenges associated with extracting natural gas from the identified reservoir.

Economic Risk: The potential return on investment, considering factors such as the cost of exploration and production, market prices, and regulatory conditions.

THE PRODUCTION PHASE

Once a natural gas reserve is deemed viable, the production phase begins. This phase involves extracting natural gas from the reservoir, processing it to remove impurities, and transporting it to market. The production phase includes several key stages:

1. DRILLING AND COMPLETION

Production drilling involves drilling multiple wells in the reservoir to extract natural gas. The process of drilling and completing a well involves several steps:

Directional Drilling: This technique allows wells to be drilled at various angles, enabling access to multiple sections of the reservoir from a single drilling site. Directional drilling is particularly useful in unconventional reservoirs, such as shale gas formations.

Hydraulic Fracturing: Commonly known as fracking, this technique involves injecting a mixture of water, sand, and chemicals into the well at high pressure to create fractures in the rock formation. These fractures allow natural gas to flow more freely into the well.

Well Completion: After drilling and fracturing, the well is completed by installing production tubing and other equipment necessary for extracting natural gas. The well is then connected to gathering lines that transport the gas to processing facilities.

2. PROCESSING AND TREATMENT

Before natural gas can be transported and sold, it must be processed and treated to remove impurities and meet market specifications. The processing phase includes:

Separation: Natural gas is often found in association with other hydrocarbons, water, and impurities. The first step in processing is to separate these components using various techniques, such as separators and dehydrators.

Conditioning: After separation, the natural gas is further treated to remove impurities, such as sulfur compounds, carbon dioxide, and water vapor. This conditioning process ensures that the gas meets the quality standards required for pipeline transport and end use.

Liquefaction: In some cases, natural gas is cooled and compressed into liquefied natural gas (LNG) for easier transport and storage. LNG occupies significantly less volume than gaseous natural gas, making it suitable for transport over long distances by ship.

3. TRANSPORTATION AND STORAGE

Once processed, natural gas is transported to consumers via pipelines, LNG tankers, or other means. Key elements of transportation and storage include:

Pipelines: Pipelines are the primary mode of transportation for natural gas, connecting production sites to processing facilities, storage facilities, and end users. Pipelines must be carefully managed and maintained to ensure safety and efficiency.

LNG Tankers: For markets that cannot be reached by pipeline, LNG is transported by specialized tankers. These tankers are designed to maintain the natural gas in a liquefied state, allowing for efficient transport across oceans.

Storage Facilities: Natural gas is stored in underground facilities to manage supply and demand fluctuations. Storage allows producers to balance production levels with market demand and ensures a reliable supply of natural gas during peak demand periods.

KEY PLAYERS IN EXPLORATION AND PRODUCTION

The exploration and production of natural gas involve a diverse range of players, each with unique roles and responsibilities. The key players in the E&P sector include:

Major Integrated Oil and Gas Companies: These companies, such as ExxonMobil, Chevron, and Shell, are involved in all aspects of the natural gas value chain, from exploration and production to refining, marketing, and distribution. They have the resources and expertise to undertake large-scale exploration and production projects.

Independent E&P Companies: Independent companies, such as Chesapeake Energy and Devon Energy, specialize in exploration and production activities. They often focus on specific regions or types of reservoirs, such as shale gas or offshore fields.

National Oil and Gas Companies (NOCs): In many countries, natural gas exploration and production are dominated by state-owned enterprises, such as Saudi Aramco in Saudi Arabia and Gazprom in Russia. NOCs often have a significant influence on national energy policies and play a key role in global natural gas markets.

Service Companies: Service companies, such as Schlumberger and Halliburton, provide the technical expertise and equipment needed for exploration and production. These companies offer a wide range of services, including drilling, well completion, seismic surveys, and reservoir management.

CHALLENGES AND OPPORTUNITIES IN EXPLORATION AND PRODUCTION

The exploration and production of natural gas come with a unique set of challenges and opportunities. Understanding these factors is crucial for navigating the complexities of the E&P sector:

1. CHALLENGES

Technical Challenges: Extracting natural gas from deep reservoirs, offshore fields, or unconventional formations, such as shale and tight gas, presents significant technical challenges. These challenges include drilling in high-pressure and high-temperature environments, managing complex reservoir geology, and ensuring the integrity of wells and pipelines.

Environmental Concerns: The E&P sector faces increasing scrutiny over its environmental impact, particularly in relation to greenhouse gas emissions, water usage, and habitat disruption. Companies must adhere to strict environmental regulations and invest in technologies that minimize their ecological footprint.

Regulatory and Political Risks: Exploration and production activities are subject to a wide range of regulations and political risks. Changes in government policies, tax regimes, or environmental regulations can significantly impact the viability of E&P projects. Companies must navigate complex regulatory environments and engage with stakeholders to mitigate these risks.

2. OPPORTUNITIES

Technological Innovations: Advances in drilling and extraction technologies, such as horizontal drilling and hydraulic fracturing, have opened up new opportunities for natural gas production. These innovations have increased the efficiency and productivity of E&P operations, reducing costs and enabling access to previously untapped resources.

Rising Demand for Natural Gas: The global demand for natural gas is expected to continue growing, driven by its use as a cleaner alternative to coal and oil. This rising demand presents significant opportunities for E&P companies to expand their operations and invest in new projects.

Expansion of LNG Markets: The growth of LNG markets provides new opportunities for natural gas producers to reach global consumers. The development of LNG export terminals and shipping infrastructure has expanded the reach of natural gas producers, allowing them to access markets in Asia, Europe, and other regions.

Exploration and production are the critical first steps in the natural gas value chain, laying the foundation for the supply of this vital energy resource. The E&P sector is characterized by its complexity, involving a diverse range of players, technical challenges, and regulatory environments. Despite these challenges, the sector offers significant opportunities for growth and innovation, driven by rising demand and technological advancements.

CHAPTER 6: TRANSPORTATION AND STORAGE

Transportation and storage are critical components of the natural gas value chain, ensuring that natural gas is efficiently delivered from production sites to end users. These processes play a vital role in balancing supply and demand, maintaining market stability, and ensuring the reliability of natural gas as an energy source. In this chapter, we will explore the infrastructure, logistics, and strategies involved in transporting and storing natural gas, as well as the challenges and opportunities that arise in these areas.

TRANSPORTATION OF NATURAL GAS

The transportation of natural gas involves moving it from production sites, such as gas fields and offshore platforms, to processing facilities, storage locations, and end-use markets. The primary modes of transportation include pipelines and liquefied natural gas (LNG) tankers.

1. PIPELINE TRANSPORTATION

Pipelines are the most common and efficient method of transporting natural gas over land. The pipeline network is vast, spanning continents and connecting producers to consumers. Key aspects of pipeline transportation include:

Pipeline Infrastructure: Natural gas pipelines are made of high-strength steel and are buried underground to protect them from external damage. The pipeline network includes gathering systems (which transport gas from production sites to processing facilities), transmission pipelines (which carry gas over long distances), and distribution pipelines (which deliver gas to homes and businesses).

Compressor Stations: Along the pipeline network, compressor stations are installed to maintain the pressure needed to move natural gas through the pipes. These stations compress the gas, boosting its pressure and allowing it to flow efficiently over long distances. Compressor stations are spaced at regular intervals along the pipeline and are critical for ensuring a steady flow of gas.

Pipeline Monitoring and Maintenance: Pipelines are continuously monitored for leaks, pressure changes, and other anomalies using advanced technologies, such as sensors, drones, and smart pigging (a method of inspecting the inside of pipelines). Regular maintenance and inspection are essential to prevent leaks, ruptures, and other safety hazards.

Cross-Border Pipelines: In many regions, natural gas pipelines cross national borders, facilitating international trade. These cross-border pipelines require coordination between countries, including agreements on tariffs, regulations, and safety standards. Notable examples include the Trans-Siberian Pipeline (linking Russia to Europe) and the TransCanada Pipeline (linking Canada to the United States).

2. LIQUEFIED NATURAL GAS (LNG) TRANSPORTATION

For regions that are not connected by pipelines, liquefied natural gas (LNG) provides an alternative method of transporting natural gas over long distances. LNG transportation involves several key steps:

Liquefaction: Natural gas is converted into LNG by cooling it to approximately -162°C (-260°F). This process reduces the volume of the gas by about 600 times, making it easier and more cost-effective to transport. Liquefaction is typically performed at export terminals located near production sites.

LNG Tankers: LNG is transported by specialized ships known as LNG tankers. These tankers are equipped with insulated tanks that keep the gas in its liquid state during transport. LNG tankers are capable of carrying large volumes of gas across oceans, connecting producers to distant markets.

Regasification: Upon arrival at the destination, LNG is regasified by heating it back to its gaseous state. This process is carried out at import terminals, where the gas is then injected into the local pipeline network for distribution to consumers.

LNG Markets: The LNG market is global, with major producers such as Qatar, Australia, and the United States exporting LNG to countries in Asia, Europe, and elsewhere. The flexibility of LNG transport allows producers to respond to changes in demand and take advantage of price differentials between regions.

STORAGE OF NATURAL GAS

Storage plays a crucial role in balancing the supply and demand of natural gas, particularly in markets with seasonal variations in consumption. Storage facilities allow excess gas to be stored during periods of low demand and withdrawn during periods of high demand. The main types of storage facilities include underground storage, LNG storage, and pipeline linepack.

1. UNDERGROUND STORAGE

Underground storage is the most common method of storing natural gas and involves injecting gas into subsurface formations. The main types of underground storage facilities are:

Depleted Gas Reservoirs: These are former natural gas fields that have been depleted of their recoverable gas reserves. Depleted reservoirs are ideal for storage because they already have the necessary geological structure and pipeline infrastructure in place. The gas is injected back into the reservoir during periods of low demand and withdrawn when demand increases.

Aquifers: Aquifers are water-bearing formations that can be used to store natural gas. The gas is injected into the aquifer and displaces the water, which acts as a pressure seal. Aquifers are typically used in regions where depleted reservoirs are not available, but they require more monitoring and maintenance than other storage types.

Salt Caverns: Salt caverns are created by dissolving underground salt deposits with water and then injecting natural gas into the resulting cavities. Salt caverns offer high deliverability, meaning they can quickly inject or withdraw large volumes of gas. This makes them ideal for managing short-term fluctuations in demand.

2. LNG STORAGE

LNG storage facilities are used to store liquefied natural gas, either for export, import, or peak-shaving (load shedding) purposes. Key aspects of LNG storage include:

LNG Terminals: LNG storage is typically located at export and import terminals. Export terminals store LNG before it is loaded onto tankers for transport, while import terminals store LNG after it has been unloaded from tankers and before it is regasified.

Peak-Shaving: In some regions, LNG is stored in peak-shaving facilities to manage short-term spikes in demand, such as during extreme cold weather. These facilities allow utilities to meet sudden increases in demand without relying on additional pipeline capacity.

3. PIPELINE LINEPACK

Pipeline linepack refers to the ability of pipelines to store a certain amount of natural gas within the pipeline system itself. By increasing or decreasing the pressure within the pipeline, operators can store or release small amounts of gas as needed. Linepack is used for short-term balancing of supply and demand and is a critical tool for maintaining the stability of the pipeline network.

CHALLENGES AND OPPORTUNITIES IN TRANSPORTATION AND STORAGE

The transportation and storage of natural gas involve complex logistics and infrastructure, and both present unique challenges and opportunities.

1. CHALLENGES

Infrastructure Investment: Developing and maintaining the infrastructure for natural gas transportation and storage requires significant investment. This includes building pipelines, LNG terminals, and storage facilities, as well as ongoing maintenance and upgrades. Securing financing and managing the costs of these projects can be challenging, particularly in regions with regulatory or political uncertainties.

Regulatory and Environmental Concerns: The construction and operation of pipelines and storage facilities are subject to a wide range of regulations, including safety standards, environmental protection, and land use. Navigating these regulations can be complex, and non-compliance can result in delays, fines, or project cancellations. Additionally, environmental concerns, such as the impact of pipeline leaks or methane emissions from storage facilities, have led to increased scrutiny and regulation.

Geopolitical Risks: Cross-border pipelines and LNG trade are subject to geopolitical risks, including trade disputes, sanctions, and conflicts. These risks can disrupt the flow of natural gas, leading to supply shortages and price volatility. Companies involved in transportation and storage must carefully assess and manage these risks to ensure the reliability of supply.

Market Dynamics: The natural gas market is highly dynamic, with prices and demand fluctuating based on factors such as weather, economic conditions, and energy policies. Transportation and storage operators must be able to adapt to these changes, optimizing their operations to take advantage of market opportunities while minimizing risks.

2. OPPORTUNITIES

Technological Advancements: Advances in technology are creating new opportunities in natural gas transportation and storage. For example, improvements in pipeline materials and monitoring systems are enhancing the safety and efficiency of pipeline networks. Similarly, innovations in LNG technology are reducing the costs and environmental impact of liquefaction and regasification processes.

Expanding Markets: The growth of global LNG markets is creating new opportunities for natural gas producers and traders. LNG's ability to reach markets that are not connected by pipelines allows companies to tap into new demand centers and diversify their customer base. This expansion is particularly important in regions such as Asia, where demand for natural gas is expected to continue growing.

Integration with Renewable Energy: Natural gas is increasingly being integrated with renewable energy sources, such as wind and solar, to provide a reliable and flexible energy supply. For example, natural gas-fired power plants can be ramped up quickly to compensate for fluctuations in renewable energy output. Storage facilities also play a critical role in balancing the intermittent nature of renewable energy, ensuring a steady supply of natural gas when needed.

Decarbonization Initiatives: As the world moves towards decarbonization, natural gas is positioned as a transition fuel, offering lower carbon emissions compared to coal and oil. Opportunities exist for the development of carbon capture and storage (CCS) technologies, which can be integrated with natural gas production and storage facilities to reduce greenhouse gas emissions. Additionally, the development of hydrogen from natural gas (with carbon capture) presents a potential future market for natural gas producers.

THE ROLE OF STORAGE IN MARKET STABILITY

Storage is a critical component of market stability in the natural gas industry. By providing a buffer between supply and demand, storage helps prevent price spikes and supply shortages. Key aspects of storage's role in market stability include:

Seasonal Balancing: Natural gas demand is often seasonal, with higher demand in the winter for heating and lower demand in the summer. Storage facilities allow natural gas to be stored during the low-demand summer months and withdrawn during the high-demand winter months, ensuring a steady supply of gas throughout the year. This seasonal balancing helps stabilize prices and reduces the risk of shortages during peak demand periods.

Peak Demand Management: In addition to seasonal fluctuations, natural gas demand can also experience short-term spikes due to extreme weather conditions, such as cold snaps or heatwaves. Storage facilities provide a critical reserve that can be quickly accessed to meet these sudden increases in demand. By injecting gas into the market during peak demand, storage operators help prevent price surges and maintain a stable supply.

Supply Disruption Mitigation: Storage plays a vital role in mitigating the impact of supply disruptions, such as pipeline outages, production declines, or geopolitical events. By maintaining strategic reserves of natural gas, storage facilities can cushion the market against unforeseen supply interruptions, reducing the risk of price volatility and supply shortages.

Price Arbitrage Opportunities: Storage also enables market participants to take advantage of price arbitrage opportunities. When prices are low, traders and producers can inject gas into storage and then withdraw and sell it when prices are higher. This practice helps smooth out price fluctuations and contributes to overall market stability.

Flexible Supply Management: Storage facilities provide flexibility in managing the supply of natural gas to different regions and markets. By storing gas close to demand centers, storage operators can quickly respond to changes in regional demand, ensuring a reliable supply of gas where and when it is needed. This flexibility is particularly important in markets with limited pipeline capacity or connectivity.

Integration with Renewable Energy: As the energy industry moves towards greater integration with renewable sources, such as wind and solar, natural gas storage will play a crucial role in balancing the intermittent nature of these energy sources. By storing excess gas during periods of high renewable energy production and releasing it during periods of low production, storage facilities can help maintain a stable and reliable energy supply.

STRATEGIES FOR EFFECTIVE TRANSPORTATION AND STORAGE

To maximize the efficiency and effectiveness of natural gas transportation and storage, market participants employ various strategies and technologies. These strategies are aimed at optimizing the use of infrastructure, minimizing costs, and enhancing the reliability of supply.

1. TRANSPORTATION STRATEGIES

Optimizing Pipeline Flows: Pipeline operators use sophisticated modeling and simulation tools to optimize the flow of natural gas through the pipeline network. By adjusting compressor station settings, pipeline pressures, and flow rates, operators can ensure that gas is delivered efficiently and reliably to meet demand.

Expanding Pipeline Capacity: To accommodate growing demand for natural gas, pipeline operators may expand the capacity of existing pipelines or construct new pipelines. These expansions are often accompanied by investments in new compressor stations, storage facilities, and other infrastructure to support the increased flow of gas.

Diversifying Transportation Modes: In addition to pipelines, market participants may use a combination of transportation modes, including LNG tankers, rail, and trucks, to transport natural gas to different markets. This diversification helps reduce reliance on a single mode of transportation and enhances the flexibility and resilience of the supply chain.

2. STORAGE STRATEGIES

Strategic Location of Storage Facilities: The location of storage facilities is a critical factor in optimizing the use of storage resources. By strategically locating storage facilities near demand centers, pipeline hubs, or production areas, market participants can minimize transportation costs and enhance the reliability of supply.

Flexible Withdrawal and Injection Schedules: Storage operators use flexible schedules for injecting gas into storage and withdrawing it for delivery to the market. By adjusting these schedules based on market conditions, storage operators can optimize the use of storage capacity and maximize the value of stored gas.

Use of Advanced Technologies: Advanced technologies, such as real-time monitoring systems, predictive analytics, and automated control systems, are used to enhance the efficiency and safety of storage operations. These technologies enable storage operators to monitor inventory levels, forecast demand, and manage injection and withdrawal rates more effectively.

Hedging and Risk Management: To manage the risks associated with price volatility and supply disruptions, market participants use a variety of financial instruments and strategies, such as futures contracts, options, and swaps. These hedging and risk management tools help storage operators and traders protect their investments and ensure a stable return on their storage assets.

The transportation and storage of natural gas are critical components of the global energy market, providing the infrastructure and flexibility needed to ensure a reliable and stable supply of natural gas. By effectively managing the transportation and storage of natural gas, market participants can optimize the use of resources, enhance market stability, and take advantage of opportunities in the dynamic natural gas market.

As the natural gas industry continues to evolve, transportation and storage will play an increasingly important role in meeting the world's energy needs. Advances in technology, changes in market dynamics, and the integration of renewable energy sources will all shape the future of natural gas transportation and storage, creating new challenges and opportunities for market participants.

CHAPTER 7: PROCESSING AND DISTRIBUTION

Processing and distribution are crucial stages in the natural gas supply chain that prepare the commodity for the market and deliver it to end users. This chapter explores the processing steps that natural gas undergoes before it is sold and the distribution systems that ensure its availability to consumers. Understanding these components is essential for anyone involved in natural gas trading, as they influence market dynamics, pricing, and the availability of gas in different regions.

PROCESSING OF NATURAL GAS

Natural gas extracted from the ground often contains impurities and non-hydrocarbon gases that must be removed to meet quality specifications and safety standards. The processing of natural gas involves several steps to ensure that it is suitable for transport and consumption.

1. REMOVAL OF IMPURITIES

The first step in natural gas processing is the removal of impurities, which can include water vapor, hydrogen sulfide, carbon dioxide, and other contaminants. This is typically achieved through the following processes:

Dehydration: Water vapor is removed from natural gas to prevent the formation of hydrates, which can clog pipelines and equipment. Dehydration is usually accomplished using desiccants, such as silica gel or molecular sieves, or through glycol dehydration, where a glycol solution absorbs the water from the gas stream.

Sweetening: Hydrogen sulfide and carbon dioxide, which are often present in natural gas, must be removed to prevent corrosion in pipelines and equipment. This process, known as sweetening, is typically performed using chemical solvents, such as amines, which absorb the sour gas components.

Nitrogen Removal: In some cases, natural gas may contain significant amounts of nitrogen, which can reduce its heating value and affect combustion. Nitrogen removal is usually carried out through cryogenic processes, where the gas is cooled to very low temperatures, allowing the nitrogen to be separated and removed.

2. SEPARATION OF NATURAL GAS LIQUIDS (NGLS)

Natural gas often contains valuable natural gas liquids (NGLs), such as ethane, propane, butane, and natural gasoline, which can be separated and sold as separate products. The separation of NGLs is typically performed using one of the following methods:

Fractionation: Fractionation is a process that separates NGLs based on their different boiling points. The gas is first cooled and compressed to condense the NGLs, and then passed through a series of fractionation columns, where the different components are separated based on their volatility.

Cryogenic Processing: Cryogenic processing is a more advanced method of separating NGLs that involves cooling the gas to extremely low temperatures, typically below -100°C (-148°F). This process allows for the efficient separation of NGLs from the gas stream, resulting in higher purity products and increased recovery rates.

3. QUALITY CONTROL AND COMPRESSION

Once the natural gas has been processed and the impurities and NGLs have been removed, it undergoes final quality control checks to ensure that it meets the specifications required for transportation and distribution. The gas is then compressed to increase its pressure, making it suitable for transport through pipelines and storage in underground facilities.

DISTRIBUTION OF NATURAL GAS

The distribution of natural gas involves delivering it from processing facilities to end users, such as residential, commercial, industrial, and power generation customers. The distribution system is a complex network of pipelines, compressor stations, and distribution centers that ensure the reliable and safe delivery of natural gas to consumers.

1. DISTRIBUTION NETWORK

The distribution network consists of several key components, each of which plays a vital role in the delivery of natural gas to consumers:

Transmission Pipelines: After processing, natural gas is transported through high-capacity transmission pipelines, which carry the gas over long distances from production areas to demand centers. These pipelines are typically operated at high pressures and are designed to handle large volumes of gas.

Compressor Stations: Along the transmission pipeline network, compressor stations are installed to maintain the pressure and flow of natural gas. These stations use large compressors to boost the gas pressure, allowing it to travel efficiently through the pipelines.

City Gate Stations: As natural gas approaches urban and suburban areas, it passes through city gate stations, where the pressure is reduced and the gas is odorized to facilitate leak detection. The gas is then directed into the local distribution network, which includes smaller pipelines that deliver gas to homes, businesses, and other end users.

Distribution Pipelines: The local distribution network consists of a complex system of pipelines that deliver natural gas to individual customers. These pipelines are typically operated at lower pressures than transmission pipelines and are designed to ensure the safe and reliable delivery of gas to consumers.

2. SAFETY AND REGULATION

The distribution of natural gas is subject to strict safety and regulatory standards to protect consumers, the environment, and the integrity of the distribution network. Key aspects of safety and regulation in the distribution of natural gas include:

Pipeline Safety Standards: Pipeline operators must adhere to strict safety standards to prevent leaks, explosions, and other incidents. These standards cover pipeline design, construction, operation, maintenance, and inspection, and are enforced by government agencies, such as the U.S. Pipeline and Hazardous Materials Safety Administration (PHMSA) and the European Union Agency for the Cooperation of Energy Regulators (ACER).

Leak Detection and Monitoring: Pipeline operators use advanced technologies, such as sensors, drones, and automated monitoring systems, to detect and respond to leaks and other anomalies in the distribution network. Regular inspections and maintenance are also carried out to ensure the integrity of the pipelines and prevent incidents.

Emergency Response and Preparedness: Pipeline operators

and local authorities work together to develop and implement emergency response plans to address potential incidents, such as pipeline ruptures or natural disasters. These plans include procedures for evacuating affected areas, shutting down pipelines, and coordinating with emergency services.

MARKET DYNAMICS AND DISTRIBUTION

The distribution of natural gas plays a critical role in the dynamics of the natural gas market, influencing prices, availability, and the overall supply-demand balance. Understanding these dynamics is essential for traders and market participants.

1. REGIONAL PRICE DIFFERENCES

The cost of transporting natural gas from production areas to demand centers can result in regional price differences, known as basis differentials. These price differences are influenced by factors such as pipeline capacity, transportation costs, and demand patterns. Traders can take advantage of these basis differentials by buying gas in low-cost regions and selling it in high-cost regions, a strategy known as basis trading.

2. IMPACT OF INFRASTRUCTURE CONSTRAINTS

Infrastructure constraints, such as limited pipeline capacity or storage availability, can have a significant impact on the distribution and pricing of natural gas. During periods of high demand or supply disruptions, these constraints can lead to price spikes and volatility in the market. Traders and market participants must closely monitor infrastructure developments and capacity constraints to effectively manage their positions and mitigate risks.

3. INFLUENCE OF REGULATORY CHANGES

Regulatory changes, such as new safety standards, environmental regulations, or market reforms, can also impact the distribution of natural gas. These changes can affect the cost of transportation, the availability of pipeline capacity, and the overall market structure. Traders and market participants must stay informed about regulatory developments and adapt their strategies accordingly.

OPPORTUNITIES AND CHALLENGES IN PROCESSING AND DISTRIBUTION

The processing and distribution of natural gas present both opportunities and challenges for market participants. Understanding these factors is essential for success in the natural gas market.

1. OPPORTUNITIES

Investment in Infrastructure: As demand for natural gas continues to grow, there are significant opportunities for investment in processing and distribution infrastructure. This includes the development of new pipelines, compressor stations, storage facilities, and processing plants, as well as the expansion and modernization of existing infrastructure.

Technological Advancements: Advances in technology are creating new opportunities for improving the efficiency, safety, and environmental performance of processing and distribution operations. For example, the use of smart pipeline monitoring systems, advanced materials, and automation technologies can enhance the reliability and resilience of the distribution network.

Integration with Renewable Energy: The integration of natural gas with renewable energy sources, such as wind and solar, offers opportunities for enhancing the flexibility and reliability of the energy supply. By using natural gas as a backup or peaking fuel, utilities can ensure a stable and reliable supply of electricity, even when renewable energy production is variable.

2. CHALLENGES

Infrastructure Constraints: One of the main challenges in the distribution of natural gas is the limited capacity of existing infrastructure to meet growing demand. In many regions, pipeline capacity and storage availability are insufficient to accommodate the increasing volumes of gas being produced and consumed. This can lead to congestion, delays, and increased costs for market participants.

Regulatory and Environmental Concerns: The processing and distribution of natural gas are subject to a wide range of regulatory and environmental requirements, which can create challenges for market participants. Compliance with these regulations can be costly and time-consuming, and failure to meet regulatory standards can result in fines, penalties, or legal action.

Geopolitical Risks: The distribution of natural gas is often influenced by geopolitical factors, such as trade disputes, sanctions, and conflicts. These risks can disrupt the flow of natural gas and affect market dynamics, creating uncertainty and volatility for traders and market participants.

Processing and distribution are essential components of the natural gas supply chain, ensuring that the gas is ready for the market and delivered to consumers in a safe and reliable manner. By understanding the processes and systems involved in processing and distribution, market participants can better anticipate market dynamics, identify opportunities, and mitigate

CHAPTER 8: THE ROLE OF INFRASTRUCTURE IN MARKET DYNAMICS

Infrastructure plays a pivotal role in shaping the dynamics of the natural gas market. From pipelines and storage facilities to processing plants and LNG terminals, the infrastructure supporting the natural gas industry determines the flow of gas, influences pricing, and affects the supply-demand balance. This chapter delves into the various types of infrastructure critical to the natural gas market and explores how they impact market dynamics, trading strategies, and investment decisions.

TYPES OF NATURAL GAS INFRASTRUCTURE

The natural gas industry relies on an extensive and complex network of infrastructure to extract, process, transport, and distribute gas to end users. Key types of infrastructure include:

1. PIPELINES

Pipelines are the primary mode of transportation for natural gas, moving it from production areas to processing facilities, storage sites, and demand centers. Pipelines are classified into three main categories:

Gathering Pipelines: These small-diameter pipelines collect natural gas from wellheads and transport it to processing facilities. Gathering pipelines are typically located in or near pro-

CHAPTER 8: THE ROLE OF INFRASTRUCTURE IN MARKET DYNAMICS

duction fields and are the first link in the natural gas supply chain.

Transmission Pipelines: These large-diameter, high-capacity pipelines transport processed natural gas over long distances, connecting production regions with major markets. Transmission pipelines are the backbone of the natural gas infrastructure, moving gas across states, regions, and even countries.

Distribution Pipelines: These smaller pipelines deliver natural gas from transmission pipelines to end users, including residential, commercial, and industrial customers. Distribution pipelines operate at lower pressures and are designed to ensure safe and reliable delivery to consumers.

2. STORAGE FACILITIES

Storage facilities play a crucial role in balancing supply and demand in the natural gas market. They allow excess gas to be stored during periods of low demand and withdrawn during periods of high demand. The main types of storage facilities include:

Underground Storage: This is the most common form of natural gas storage, involving the injection of gas into underground formations, such as depleted oil and gas fields, aquifers, and salt caverns. Underground storage provides a large capacity for long-term storage and is essential for managing seasonal fluctuations in demand.

Liquefied Natural Gas (LNG) Storage: LNG storage involves cooling natural gas to a liquid state, reducing its volume for easier storage and transportation. LNG storage facilities are often located near LNG export terminals, regasification plants, and major markets, providing flexibility in meeting peak demand or serving remote regions.

3. LIQUEFIED NATURAL GAS (LNG) INFRASTRUCTURE

LNG infrastructure is critical for transporting natural gas across long distances, particularly to markets that are not connected by pipelines. Key components of LNG infrastructure include:

Liquefaction Plants: These facilities cool natural gas to approximately -162°C (-260°F), converting it into a liquid form that can be transported by ship. Liquefaction plants are typically located near natural gas production areas or at ports with access to shipping routes.

LNG Terminals: LNG terminals are facilities where LNG is received, stored, and regasified (converted back into a gaseous state) for distribution to consumers. Terminals are strategically located near major demand centers, allowing for the efficient delivery of natural gas to markets.

LNG Carriers: LNG carriers are specialized ships designed to transport LNG across oceans. These vessels are equipped with insulated tanks that keep the LNG at its low temperature during transit, allowing it to be safely delivered to distant markets.

4. PROCESSING PLANTS

Natural gas processing plants are essential for removing impurities and separating valuable components, such as natural gas liquids (NGLs). These plants ensure that natural gas meets quality specifications and is suitable for transportation and consumption. Key functions of processing plants include:

Dehydration: Removing water vapor from natural gas to prevent pipeline corrosion and hydrate formation.

Sweetening: Removing hydrogen sulfide and carbon dioxide to prevent corrosion and meet quality standards.

NGL Separation: Extracting NGLs, such as ethane, propane, and butane, which can be sold separately or used as feedstock for petrochemical production.

IMPACT OF INFRASTRUCTURE ON MARKET DYNAMICS

The availability, capacity, and location of infrastructure have a profound impact on the natural gas market. These factors influence the flow of gas, regional price differentials, and the overall supply-demand balance.

1. PIPELINE CAPACITY AND BOTTLENECKS

Pipeline capacity is a critical factor in determining the flow of natural gas between regions. When pipeline capacity is limited or constrained, it can create bottlenecks that restrict the movement of gas, leading to regional supply shortages and price spikes. Key considerations include:

Congestion and Flow Restrictions: Congestion occurs when demand for pipeline capacity exceeds available supply, leading to flow restrictions and higher transportation costs. This can result in price differentials between regions, known as basis differentials, which traders can exploit through basis trading strategies.

Infrastructure Expansion: Expanding pipeline capacity, either through new construction or upgrades to existing infrastructure, can alleviate bottlenecks and enhance market efficiency. However, infrastructure projects are often subject to regulatory approvals, environmental concerns, and financing challenges, which can delay or limit their impact on the market.

2. STORAGE AVAILABILITY AND UTILIZATION

The availability and utilization of storage facilities are crucial for managing supply and demand in the natural gas market. Storage provides a buffer that helps stabilize prices and ensures a reliable supply of gas during periods of high demand or supply disruptions. Key factors include:

Seasonal Storage: Storage is particularly important for managing seasonal fluctuations in demand, such as increased heating needs in the winter. By storing gas during the low-demand summer months, market participants can ensure an adequate supply during the winter, preventing price spikes and supply shortages.

Strategic Reserves: In addition to seasonal storage, strategic reserves of natural gas are maintained by some countries to enhance energy security and mitigate the impact of supply disruptions, such as geopolitical events or natural disasters.

3. LNG INFRASTRUCTURE AND GLOBAL TRADE

LNG infrastructure plays a critical role in enabling global trade in natural gas, connecting markets that are not linked by pipelines. The growth of LNG infrastructure has transformed the natural gas market, creating a more interconnected and flexible global market. Key considerations include:

Global Price Convergence: The expansion of LNG trade has contributed to greater price convergence between regional markets, as LNG allows gas to be transported from regions with low prices to those with higher prices. This has reduced the price differentials between markets, creating a more unified global market.

Flexibility and Arbitrage: LNG provides flexibility in sourcing and delivering natural gas, allowing market participants to take advantage of price arbitrage opportunities. For example,

LNG can be redirected to different markets based on changing demand patterns or price signals, enhancing market efficiency and creating opportunities for traders.

4. INFRASTRUCTURE RESILIENCE AND RISK MANAGEMENT

The resilience of natural gas infrastructure is critical for ensuring a reliable and stable supply of gas. Infrastructure disruptions, whether due to natural disasters, accidents, or geopolitical events, can have significant impacts on the market, creating volatility and uncertainty. Key considerations include:

Risk Mitigation: Market participants must closely monitor infrastructure risks and implement strategies to mitigate potential disruptions. This can include diversifying supply sources, securing alternative transportation routes, and maintaining strategic reserves.

Investment in Resilience: Investment in resilient infrastructure, such as upgrading aging pipelines, enhancing storage capacity, and improving monitoring and maintenance practices, is essential for reducing the risk of disruptions and ensuring long-term market stability.

INFRASTRUCTURE INVESTMENT AND MARKET OPPORTUNITIES

Investment in natural gas infrastructure presents significant opportunities for market participants, including developers, investors, and traders. Understanding the factors driving infrastructure investment and the potential returns is essential for capitalizing on these opportunities.

1. DRIVERS OF INFRASTRUCTURE INVESTMENT

Several factors drive investment in natural gas infrastructure, including:

Demand Growth: Rising demand for natural gas, driven by factors such as economic growth, population increases, and the transition to cleaner energy sources, creates the need for expanded infrastructure to meet market needs.

Regulatory Support: Government policies and regulatory incentives, such as tax credits, subsidies, and streamlined permitting processes, can encourage investment in new infrastructure projects, particularly those that support energy security, environmental goals, or economic development.

Technological Advancements: Advances in technology, such as improved pipeline materials, more efficient processing methods, and enhanced monitoring and control systems, can reduce the costs and risks associated with infrastructure projects, making them more attractive to investors.

2. INVESTMENT OPPORTUNITIES

Key investment opportunities in natural gas infrastructure include:

Pipeline Expansion and Upgrades: Investing in the construction of new pipelines or the expansion and modernization of existing pipelines can enhance market connectivity, reduce bottlenecks, and create opportunities for arbitrage and trading.

LNG Infrastructure Development: The growth of the global LNG market presents opportunities for investment in liquefaction plants, LNG terminals, and LNG carriers, as well as associated infrastructure, such as storage facilities and regasification plants.

Storage Capacity Expansion: Expanding storage capacity, particularly in regions with significant seasonal demand fluctuations or infrastructure constraints, can provide valuable flexibility and enhance market stability, creating opportunities for storage operators and traders.

Renewable Integration: As the energy market increasingly integrates renewable energy sources, there are opportunities for investment in infrastructure that supports the flexible use of natural gas, such as gas-fired power plants, energy storage systems, and hybrid renewable-gas solutions.

As the global demand for natural gas continues to grow, the development and modernization of infrastructure will be essential for meeting market needs and ensuring a stable and resilient supply. Investment in infrastructure will not only support the expansion of the natural gas industry but also contribute to broader energy security, economic development, and environmental goals.

For traders and market participants, understanding the role of infrastructure in the natural gas market is crucial for identifying and capitalizing on opportunities. By closely monitoring infrastructure developments, capacity constraints, and regulatory changes, traders can better anticipate market dynamics, manage risks, and develop strategies that maximize their returns.

PART 3: NATURAL GAS PRICING AND MARKET STRUCTURES

CHAPTER 9: UNDERSTANDING SPOT AND FUTURES MARKETS

The natural gas market comprises two primary trading arenas: the spot market and the futures market. Understanding the characteristics, functions, and dynamics of these markets is crucial for anyone looking to trade natural gas or invest in this energy sector. This chapter explores the key features of the spot and futures markets, their roles in the natural gas industry, and the strategies traders use to navigate these markets effectively.

THE SPOT MARKET

The spot market, also known as the cash market or physical market, is where natural gas is bought and sold for immediate delivery. Transactions in the spot market are typically settled "on the spot," with physical delivery occurring within a short period, usually a few days. The spot market is characterized by its volatility and responsiveness to short-term supply and demand dynamics.

1. CHARACTERISTICS OF THE SPOT MARKET

Short-Term Trading: Spot market transactions are based on current market conditions, with prices reflecting the immediate supply and demand balance. This makes the spot market highly sensitive to fluctuations in factors such as weather, production levels, and infrastructure constraints.

Price Volatility: Prices in the spot market can vary significantly over short periods due to unexpected changes in supply or demand. For example, a sudden cold snap in winter can lead to a surge in demand for heating, driving up spot prices. Conversely, a temporary increase in production or a reduction in demand can cause spot prices to drop.

Regional Variations: Spot prices can differ between regions based on local supply and demand conditions, pipeline capacity, and transportation costs. These regional price differences, known as basis differentials, create opportunities for arbitrage and basis trading strategies.

2. ROLE OF THE SPOT MARKET

The spot market plays a vital role in the natural gas industry by providing a mechanism for balancing short-term supply and demand. Key functions of the spot market include:

Price Discovery: The spot market is a primary source of price discovery for natural gas, reflecting the real-time balance of supply and demand. Spot prices serve as a benchmark for other pricing mechanisms, including long-term contracts and futures markets.

Liquidity and Flexibility: The spot market provides liquidity and flexibility for market participants, allowing them to adjust their positions based on changing market conditions. Producers, consumers, and traders can use the spot market to manage their exposure to price risks and secure supplies or sales as needed.

Arbitrage Opportunities: The spot market creates opportunities for arbitrage, where traders can exploit price differences between regions or between the spot and futures markets. By buying gas in a lower-priced market and selling it in a higher-priced market, traders can profit from these price differentials.

THE FUTURES MARKET

The futures market is a financial market where participants buy and sell contracts for the future delivery of natural gas. Futures contracts are standardized agreements to buy or sell a specified quantity of natural gas at a predetermined price and date. The futures market is characterized by its ability to provide price transparency, risk management, and speculative opportunities.

1. CHARACTERISTICS OF THE FUTURES MARKET

Standardization: Futures contracts are standardized in terms of quantity, quality, delivery location, and delivery date. This standardization makes futures contracts easily tradable and facilitates price comparison and market liquidity.

Leverage: Futures trading allows participants to control large positions with a relatively small amount of capital, known as margin. This leverage amplifies both potential profits and losses, making futures trading a high-risk, high-reward endeavor.

Hedging and Speculation: The futures market is used by a wide range of participants, including producers, consumers, and speculators. Producers and consumers use futures contracts to hedge against price risks, while speculators seek to profit from price movements by taking long or short positions in the market.

2. ROLE OF THE FUTURES MARKET

The futures market serves several important functions in the natural gas industry, including:

Price Discovery: Futures prices provide a forward-looking view of the market's expectations for natural gas prices. By reflecting the collective outlook of market participants, futures prices offer valuable information for producers, consumers, and investors.

Risk Management: Futures contracts allow market participants to hedge against price risks by locking in prices for future deliveries. For example, a natural gas producer can sell futures contracts to secure a fixed price for their production, protecting against potential price declines.

Speculation and Arbitrage: The futures market offers opportunities for speculation and arbitrage, where traders can profit from anticipated price movements or price discrepancies between the spot and futures markets. Speculative trading adds liquidity to the market and contributes to price efficiency.

STRATEGIES FOR TRADING IN THE SPOT AND FUTURES MARKETS

Trading in the spot and futures markets requires a deep understanding of market dynamics, pricing mechanisms, and risk management. Several strategies can be employed by traders to navigate these markets effectively.

1. SPOT MARKET STRATEGIES

Day Trading: Day traders seek to profit from short-term price movements in the spot market by buying and selling natural gas within the same trading day. This strategy requires quick decision-making and a keen understanding of market indicators and trends.

Spread Trading: Spread trading involves taking positions in different regional spot markets to exploit price differentials. For example, a trader might buy gas in a lower-priced market and sell it in a higher-priced market, capturing the price spread as profit.

Weather-Based Trading: Weather conditions have a significant impact on natural gas demand, particularly for heating and cooling. Traders can use weather forecasts and data to anticipate changes in demand and adjust their positions accordingly.

2. FUTURES MARKET STRATEGIES

Hedging: Producers, consumers, and other market participants use futures contracts to hedge against price risks. By taking positions in the futures market that offset their physical positions, they can lock in prices and reduce their exposure to market volatility.

Speculative Trading: Speculators use various strategies to profit from anticipated price movements in the futures market. These strategies include trend following, mean reversion, and technical analysis.

Options Trading: In addition to futures contracts, traders can use options contracts to speculate on or hedge against price movements. Options provide the right, but not the obligation, to buy or sell futures contracts at a specified price and date, offering flexibility and risk management.

The spot and futures markets are integral components of the natural gas industry, providing mechanisms for price discovery, risk management, and speculative opportunities. Understanding the characteristics and functions of these markets is essential for anyone looking to trade natural gas or invest in the energy sector. By developing a solid understanding of market dynamics and employing effective trading strategies, traders and investors can navigate the complexities of the spot and futures markets and capitalize on opportunities in the natural gas market.

CHAPTER 10: PRICING HUBS AND BENCHMARKS

In the natural gas market, pricing hubs and benchmarks are essential tools for determining and standardizing gas prices. These mechanisms facilitate transparent pricing, enable effective trading, and support market participants in managing their financial and operational risks. This chapter explores the key pricing hubs and benchmarks in the natural gas market, their roles in price formation, and how traders use them to inform their strategies.

WHAT ARE PRICING HUBS?

Pricing hubs are specific locations or trading points where natural gas prices are determined and reported. These hubs serve as reference points for market participants to buy or sell natural gas, and they play a crucial role in establishing market prices through supply and demand interactions.

1. CHARACTERISTICS OF PRICING HUBS

Market Liquidity: Pricing hubs are typically located in regions with high market liquidity, meaning there is a significant volume of trading activity. This liquidity ensures that prices at these hubs reflect the true market value of natural gas.

Regional Influence: Prices at a hub can influence and be influenced by regional supply and demand conditions. Hubs often serve as key pricing points for the surrounding areas, impacting regional and even national market prices.

Transparency: Pricing hubs provide transparency in the natural gas market by offering publicly available price data. This transparency helps market participants make informed decisions and ensures fair trading practices.

2. MAJOR PRICING HUBS

Henry Hub (HH): Located in Erath, Louisiana, Henry Hub is the most widely recognized pricing hub in the United States. It serves as the primary benchmark for natural gas futures trading on the New York Mercantile Exchange (NYMEX) and is a key reference point for North American natural gas prices.

Nymex Natural Gas Hub: Also known as the New York Mercantile Exchange (NYMEX) hub, this pricing point is used for trading natural gas futures contracts. It provides a benchmark for prices and helps facilitate trading in the futures market.

Chicago Citygate: A major pricing hub in the Midwest, the Chicago Citygate is a critical point for natural gas trading in the region. Prices at this hub reflect the local supply and demand conditions and are used for regional pricing and trading.

Transco Zone 6: Located in the northeastern United States, Transco Zone 6 is a significant hub for natural gas pricing in the region. It serves as a reference point for prices in the densely populated and energy-intensive northeastern markets.

WHAT ARE BENCHMARKS?

Benchmarks are standardized reference prices used to evaluate and compare natural gas prices across different markets and contracts. They provide a consistent and reliable basis for pricing and trading, enabling market participants to assess the value of natural gas and manage their risks.

1. CHARACTERISTICS OF BENCHMARKS

Standardization: Benchmarks are standardized to ensure consistency and comparability. They are typically defined by specific contract terms, delivery points, and quality specifications, making them reliable indicators of market prices.

Market Acceptance: Benchmarks are widely accepted and used by market participants, including producers, consumers, traders, and investors. Their broad acceptance ensures that they accurately reflect market conditions and serve as reliable pricing references.

Pricing Transparency: Benchmarks provide transparency in the natural gas market by offering a clear and standardized pricing reference. This transparency helps market participants make informed decisions and supports fair trading practices.

2. MAJOR BENCHMARKS

Henry Hub Natural Gas Futures Contract: The Henry Hub futures contract, traded on the NYMEX, is the most widely used benchmark for natural gas prices in North America. It represents the delivery of natural gas at the Henry Hub pricing point and serves as the standard reference for futures trading and price reporting.

Dutch Title Transfer Facility (TTF): The TTF is a key benchmark for natural gas prices in Europe. It represents the virtual trading point for natural gas in the Netherlands and is widely used for pricing and trading natural gas across European markets.

National Balancing Point (NBP): The NBP is another important benchmark for natural gas prices in the United Kingdom. It represents the virtual trading point for natural gas in the UK and is used for pricing and trading in the British gas market.

Japan Korea Marker (JKM): The JKM is a benchmark for liquefied natural gas (LNG) prices in Asia. It represents the price of LNG delivered to Japan and Korea and is widely used for pricing and trading LNG contracts in the Asian market.

THE ROLE OF PRICING HUBS AND BENCHMARKS IN TRADING

Pricing hubs and benchmarks play a crucial role in the natural gas market by providing standardized pricing references and facilitating transparent trading. They support market participants in managing their financial and operational risks and inform trading strategies.

1. PRICE DISCOVERY

Pricing hubs and benchmarks are essential for price discovery, helping to establish the market value of natural gas. By reflecting the interactions of supply and demand, they provide accurate and timely information on market prices, enabling traders to make informed decisions.

2. RISK MANAGEMENT

Benchmarks and pricing hubs help market participants manage their financial risks by providing standardized reference prices. Traders and investors use these references to hedge their positions, assess market conditions, and develop strategies for managing price volatility.

3. ARBITRAGE OPPORTUNITIES

The existence of multiple pricing hubs and benchmarks creates opportunities for arbitrage, where traders can exploit price differentials between markets. By buying gas at a lower-priced hub and selling it at a higher-priced hub, traders can profit from these price discrepancies.

4. CONTRACT VALUATION

Benchmarks and pricing hubs are used to value natural gas contracts and determine settlement prices. They provide a consistent basis for evaluating contract terms, pricing structures, and market conditions, ensuring fairness and accuracy in contract settlements.

Pricing hubs and benchmarks are fundamental components of the natural gas market, providing standardized pricing references and facilitating transparent trading. Understanding these mechanisms is crucial for market participants looking to navigate the complexities of natural gas trading, manage their risks, and capitalize on opportunities. By leveraging pricing hubs and benchmarks, traders and investors can make informed decisions, develop effective trading strategies, and succeed in the dynamic world of natural gas markets.

CHAPTER 11: FACTORS INFLUENCING NATURAL GAS PRICES

Natural gas prices are influenced by a complex interplay of factors that affect supply and demand, market dynamics, and broader economic conditions. Understanding these factors is essential for anyone looking to trade natural gas or invest in the energy sector. This chapter explores the key factors that drive natural gas prices and their implications for market participants.

SUPPLY FACTORS

The supply side of the natural gas market encompasses various elements that affect the availability of gas. Key supply factors include:

1. PRODUCTION LEVELS

Domestic Production: The amount of natural gas produced domestically has a direct impact on prices. Increases in production can lead to lower prices due to a surplus of supply, while decreases can drive prices higher due to supply constraints.

Technological Advancements: Innovations in extraction technologies, such as hydraulic fracturing (fracking) and horizontal drilling, have significantly increased natural gas production, particularly from shale formations. These advancements can lead to more abundant supplies and influence price trends.

2. EXPLORATION AND DEVELOPMENT

New Discoveries: Discoveries of new natural gas reserves can enhance supply and potentially lower prices. Conversely, the lack of significant new discoveries can limit supply growth and contribute to higher prices.

Investment in Infrastructure: Investment in exploration and development infrastructure, such as drilling rigs and production facilities, can impact the ability to increase supply. Delays or reductions in investment can constrain supply and drive up prices.

3. IMPORT AND EXPORT DYNAMICS

LNG Imports and Exports: The trade of liquefied natural gas (LNG) can influence domestic prices by balancing supply and demand across different regions. Increased LNG exports can reduce domestic supply and raise prices, while higher imports can increase supply and potentially lower prices.

Pipeline Imports: The flow of natural gas through pipelines from other countries can also impact domestic prices. Changes in pipeline capacity or disruptions in international supply can affect the availability and cost of natural gas.

DEMAND FACTORS

Demand factors reflect the consumption of natural gas and can significantly impact prices. Key demand factors include:

1. WEATHER CONDITIONS

Seasonal Variations: Natural gas demand is highly sensitive to weather conditions. Cold winters can lead to increased demand for heating, driving up prices, while mild winters can reduce demand and lower prices. Similarly, hot summers can boost demand for cooling.

Extreme Weather Events: Severe weather events, such as hurricanes or heatwaves, can disrupt supply and infrastructure, leading to price spikes due to supply shortages or increased demand.

2. ECONOMIC ACTIVITY

Industrial and Commercial Demand: Economic growth and industrial activity can drive higher demand for natural gas as fuel for manufacturing and energy production. Strong economic performance typically leads to increased gas consumption and upward pressure on prices.

Economic Recession: Conversely, economic downturns can reduce demand for natural gas as industrial and commercial activities decline, leading to lower prices.

3. ENERGY SUBSTITUTION

Fuel Switching: The availability and cost of alternative energy sources, such as coal, oil, or renewable energy, can influence natural gas demand. If other energy sources become more competitive, demand for natural gas may decrease, affecting prices.

Policy and Regulation: Government policies and regulations that promote or restrict the use of natural gas can impact demand. For example, regulations favoring cleaner energy sources can increase demand for natural gas as a transition fuel, while policies promoting renewable energy can reduce gas consumption.

MARKET DYNAMICS

Market dynamics include factors that affect how natural gas is traded and priced in the market. Key market dynamics include:

1. STORAGE LEVELS

Inventory Levels: The amount of natural gas in storage plays a crucial role in price formation. High inventory levels can indicate a surplus of supply and exert downward pressure on prices, while low inventory levels can signal tight supply and drive prices higher.

Seasonal Storage Patterns: Natural gas storage levels typically fluctuate with seasonal demand patterns. High storage levels during the summer can help meet winter demand and stabilize prices, while low storage levels can contribute to price volatility.

2. PIPELINE AND TRANSPORTATION CONSTRAINTS

Infrastructure Capacity: The capacity of pipelines and transportation infrastructure can impact the flow of natural gas and influence prices. Bottlenecks or constraints in transportation can lead to regional price differentials and affect overall market prices.

Maintenance and Disruptions: Scheduled maintenance or unexpected disruptions to pipeline infrastructure can affect the availability of natural gas and contribute to price volatility.

3. MARKET SPECULATION

Futures and Options Trading: Speculative trading in futures and options markets can impact natural gas prices by influencing market expectations and sentiment. Large positions or changes in trading activity can create price fluctuations or amplify market trends.

Investor Sentiment: Market participants' perceptions of future supply and demand conditions can influence trading decisions and affect prices. Positive or negative news about the natural gas market can lead to speculative price movements.

11.4 GLOBAL INFLUENCES

Natural gas prices are also influenced by global factors that affect supply, demand, and market dynamics on an international scale.

1. INTERNATIONAL TRADE POLICIES

Tariffs and Trade Agreements: International trade policies, such as tariffs on LNG imports or trade agreements between countries, can impact the flow of natural gas and influence global prices. Changes in trade policies can affect supply chains and pricing dynamics.

2. GEOPOLITICAL EVENTS

Political Stability: Geopolitical events, such as conflicts, sanctions, or political instability in major natural gas-producing regions, can disrupt supply and contribute to price volatility. Market participants closely monitor geopolitical developments to assess potential risks and impacts on prices.

Global Energy Policies: International agreements and policies aimed at addressing climate change and promoting renewable energy can influence natural gas demand and pricing. Global efforts to reduce carbon emissions can impact the role of natural gas in the energy mix.

Understanding the factors influencing natural gas prices is essential for traders and investors seeking to navigate the complexities of the market. By analyzing supply and demand dynamics, market conditions, and global influences, market participants can make informed decisions, manage risks, and capitalize on opportunities in the natural gas market. A comprehensive understanding of these factors enables traders to develop effective strategies and respond to changing market conditions.

CHAPTER 12: MARKET DEREGULATION AND ITS IMPACT

Market deregulation has profoundly transformed the natural gas industry, introducing competition, increasing efficiency, and altering market dynamics. This chapter explores the concept of market deregulation, its historical context, and its impact on natural gas pricing, trading, and industry practices.

UNDERSTANDING MARKET DEREGULATION

Market deregulation refers to the process of reducing or eliminating government controls and regulations that restrict competition and market operations. In the natural gas industry, deregulation involves opening up the market to competition, allowing multiple players to participate, and promoting a more market-driven pricing mechanism.

1. HISTORICAL CONTEXT

Pre-Deregulation Era: Prior to deregulation, the natural gas industry was largely regulated, with prices and market operations controlled by government agencies. This regulatory framework was designed to protect consumers and ensure stable supply but often led to inefficiencies and a lack of competition.

Deregulation Initiatives: In the late 20th century, many countries, including the United States, began to deregulate their natural gas markets. Key legislative and regulatory changes, such as the Natural Gas Policy Act of 1978 and the Energy Policy Act of 1992 in the U.S., aimed to promote competition, increase market efficiency, and encourage investment.

2. KEY COMPONENTS OF DEREGULATION

Unbundling: Deregulation often involves unbundling, where different aspects of the natural gas supply chain—such as production, transportation, and distribution—are separated into distinct entities. This separation allows for increased competition and prevents monopolistic practices.

Open Access: Open access policies require pipeline operators to provide non-discriminatory access to their infrastructure for all market participants. This promotes competition by allowing producers, traders, and consumers to use existing transportation networks.

Market-Based Pricing: Deregulation introduces market-based pricing mechanisms, where prices are determined by supply and demand dynamics rather than being set by regulators. This shift aims to reflect the true market value of natural gas and enhance pricing efficiency.

IMPACT ON NATURAL GAS PRICING

The deregulation of the natural gas market has had significant effects on pricing, leading to both opportunities and challenges for market participants.

1. PRICE VOLATILITY

Increased Volatility: With deregulation, natural gas prices have become more volatile, reflecting real-time supply and demand conditions. Market-driven pricing can lead to sharper price fluctuations compared to regulated environments.

Price Discovery: Deregulation has enhanced the price discovery process by allowing market participants to respond quickly to changes in supply and demand. Prices are now more responsive to market conditions and reflect a wider range of factors influencing the market.

2. REGIONAL PRICE DIFFERENCES

Regional Pricing: Deregulation has led to greater regional price differences due to variations in local supply and demand conditions. Pricing hubs and benchmarks now reflect these regional differences, providing insights into localized market dynamics.

Arbitrage Opportunities: Regional price differentials create opportunities for arbitrage, where traders can exploit price differences between regions. This can lead to increased trading activity and greater market efficiency.

IMPACT ON TRADING AND MARKET PARTICIPATION

Deregulation has transformed the trading landscape, altering how natural gas is bought, sold, and managed. Key impacts include:

1. INCREASED COMPETITION

Market Entry: Deregulation has lowered barriers to entry, allowing new players to enter the market and compete with established firms. This increased competition has led to more diverse market offerings and improved services for consumers.

Innovative Trading Practices: The introduction of competition has spurred innovation in trading practices, including the use of advanced trading strategies, financial instruments, and technology to manage risks and optimize trading outcomes.

2. ENHANCED TRANSPARENCY

Price Transparency: Market deregulation has improved price transparency by providing more frequent and detailed price information. This transparency helps market participants make informed decisions and fosters a more competitive environment.

Market Data: The availability of comprehensive market data, including pricing hubs, benchmarks, and trading volumes, has enhanced market participants' ability to analyze trends, assess risks, and develop trading strategies.

CHALLENGES AND CONSIDERATIONS

While deregulation has brought numerous benefits, it has also introduced challenges and considerations for market participants.

1. RISK MANAGEMENT

Increased Risk: The shift to market-based pricing has increased the level of risk for market participants. Price volatility and market fluctuations require effective risk management strategies to mitigate potential losses and protect investments.

Hedging Strategies: Traders and investors need to employ sophisticated hedging strategies to manage exposure to price fluctuations. Futures, options, and other financial instruments are commonly used to hedge risks and stabilize returns.

2. REGULATORY ADJUSTMENTS

Evolving Regulations: Despite deregulation, some regulatory oversight remains to ensure market integrity and prevent anti-competitive practices. Market participants must stay informed about regulatory changes and comply with relevant guidelines and standards.

Regulatory Balance: Finding the right balance between deregulation and regulation is crucial to maintaining a competitive and efficient market while safeguarding consumer interests and ensuring market stability.

Market deregulation has significantly reshaped the natural gas industry, introducing competition, enhancing transparency, and altering pricing dynamics. Understanding the impact of deregulation is essential for traders and investors seeking to navigate the complexities of the market and capitalize on new opportunities. By adapting to the evolving market landscape and employing effective risk management strategies, market participants can thrive in the competitive and dynamic world of natural gas trading.

PART 4: INTRODUCTION TO NATURAL GAS TRADING INSTRUMENTS

CHAPTER 13: SPOT CONTRACTS

Spot contracts are a fundamental aspect of natural gas trading, providing a mechanism for buying and selling natural gas for immediate delivery. Understanding spot contracts is essential for navigating the natural gas market, as they reflect the current market conditions and pricing dynamics. This chapter explores the nature of spot contracts, their role in the natural gas market, and key considerations for trading them.

WHAT ARE SPOT CONTRACTS?

Spot contracts are agreements to buy or sell natural gas for immediate delivery, typically within a short timeframe, such as the next day or within a few days. The price agreed upon in a spot contract reflects the current market value of natural gas and is based on real-time supply and demand conditions.

1. KEY CHARACTERISTICS OF SPOT CONTRACTS

Immediate Delivery: Spot contracts involve the delivery of natural gas in the immediate or near-term future. The delivery schedule is usually specified in the contract, with transactions occurring promptly after the agreement.

Market Pricing: The price of natural gas in a spot contract is determined by the current market price, which fluctuates based on supply and demand dynamics. Spot prices can be more volatile than futures prices due to short-term market conditions.

Short-Term Nature: Spot contracts are short-term agreements, typically covering a delivery period of one month or less. This short-term nature allows market participants to respond quickly to changing market conditions.

ROLE OF SPOT CONTRACTS IN THE NATURAL GAS MARKET

Spot contracts play a crucial role in the natural gas market by providing a mechanism for real-time trading and price discovery. Key roles include:

1. PRICE DISCOVERY

Real-Time Pricing: Spot contracts reflect the current market value of natural gas, providing a real-time snapshot of supply and demand conditions. This real-time pricing helps market participants gauge the value of natural gas and make informed trading decisions.

Market Efficiency: By facilitating immediate transactions, spot contracts contribute to market efficiency. They enable market participants to adjust their positions based on current market conditions and help balance supply and demand.

2. SUPPLY AND DEMAND BALANCING

Short-Term Adjustments: Spot contracts allow for short-term adjustments in supply and demand. When market conditions change rapidly, such as during extreme weather events or supply disruptions, spot contracts provide a mechanism for quickly addressing imbalances.

Inventory Management: Producers and consumers use spot contracts to manage their inventories and ensure a continuous supply of natural gas. Spot trading helps meet short-term needs and align supply with consumption.

SPOT MARKET PARTICIPANTS

Various market participants engage in spot trading to meet their immediate needs and capitalize on market opportunities. Key participants include:

1. PRODUCERS

Selling Surplus: Natural gas producers use spot contracts to sell surplus gas that exceeds their contractual obligations or production forecasts. Spot trading allows producers to monetize excess production and respond to market demand.

Adjusting Production: Producers may use spot markets to adjust their production levels based on current prices and market conditions. Spot trading provides flexibility in managing production and sales strategies.

2. CONSUMERS

Meeting Immediate Needs: Consumers, including utilities and industrial users, use spot contracts to secure immediate supplies of natural gas to meet their short-term consumption needs. Spot contracts help ensure a steady supply during periods of high demand.

Price Optimization: Consumers may engage in spot trading to take advantage of favorable market prices. By purchasing natural gas through spot contracts, consumers can optimize their procurement costs and manage their budgets more effectively.

3. TRADERS AND INTERMEDIARIES

Arbitrage Opportunities: Traders and intermediaries participate in spot markets to exploit arbitrage opportunities between different pricing hubs or regions. Spot trading allows them to capitalize on price differentials and generate profits.

Market Liquidity: Traders contribute to market liquidity by buying and selling natural gas in the spot market. Their activities help facilitate efficient trading and improve market functioning.

PRICING AND SETTLEMENT

Spot contract prices are determined based on supply and demand dynamics and are typically reported by pricing hubs or benchmarks. Key aspects of pricing and settlement include:

1. SPOT PRICE DETERMINATION

Market Transactions: Spot prices are derived from actual market transactions and reflect the current supply and demand conditions at the time of the trade. Prices can vary between different pricing hubs and regions based on local market factors.

Price Reporting: Spot prices are reported by various market sources, including pricing agencies and trading platforms. These reports provide transparency and help market participants assess current market conditions.

2. SETTLEMENT AND DELIVERY

Settlement Terms: The settlement terms of spot contracts specify the payment and delivery arrangements for the traded gas. These terms are typically outlined in the contract and may include details such as payment timing, delivery location, and quantity.

Delivery Mechanisms: Delivery of natural gas under spot contracts is typically facilitated through existing transportation infrastructure, such as pipelines or LNG terminals. The delivery mechanisms are specified in the contract and may involve physical delivery or financial settlement.

13.5 RISKS AND CONSIDERATIONS

Trading spot contracts involves several risks and considerations that market participants should be aware of:

1. PRICE VOLATILITY

Market Fluctuations: Spot prices can be highly volatile due to short-term market fluctuations, supply disruptions, or unexpected demand changes. Traders and consumers need to be prepared for price swings and manage their exposure accordingly.

Risk Management: Effective risk management strategies, such as hedging and diversification, are essential for mitigating the impact of price volatility. Participants should use appropriate tools and techniques to manage their risk exposure.

2. CONTRACT TERMS AND CONDITIONS

Negotiation and Clarity: Clear negotiation and understanding of contract terms are crucial for successful spot trading. Participants should ensure that contract terms, including delivery schedules, payment arrangements, and quality specifications, are well-defined and agreed upon.

Dispute Resolution: Disputes may arise over contract terms, delivery issues, or pricing discrepancies. Participants should have procedures in place for resolving disputes and addressing potential conflicts.

Spot contracts are a vital component of the natural gas market, providing a mechanism for immediate trading and price discovery. By understanding the nature of spot contracts, their role in the market, and the associated risks and considerations, traders and consumers can effectively navigate the natural gas market and make informed decisions. Spot trading offers opportunities to respond to real-time market conditions, optimize procurement strategies, and manage short-term supply and demand imbalances.

CHAPTER 14: FUTURES CONTRACTS

Futures contracts are a cornerstone of natural gas trading, providing a mechanism for buying and selling natural gas at a predetermined price for future delivery. These contracts play a crucial role in managing price risk, speculating on future price movements, and ensuring market liquidity. This chapter delves into the concept of futures contracts, their mechanics, and their impact on the natural gas market.

WHAT ARE FUTURES CONTRACTS?

A futures contract is a standardized financial agreement to buy or sell a specified quantity of natural gas at a predetermined price on a future date. Futures contracts are traded on exchanges and are used by market participants to hedge against price fluctuations, speculate on price movements, and manage their exposure to the natural gas market.

1. KEY CHARACTERISTICS OF FUTURES CONTRACTS

Standardization: Futures contracts are standardized in terms of contract size, delivery date, and quality specifications. This standardization ensures uniformity and facilitates trading on exchanges.

Leverage: Futures contracts often involve leverage, allowing traders to control a large amount of natural gas with a relatively small margin. This leverage can amplify both potential gains and losses.

Settlement: Futures contracts can be settled either through physical delivery of natural gas or through a cash settlement, depending on the terms of the contract and the preferences of the parties involved.

ROLE OF FUTURES CONTRACTS IN THE NATURAL GAS MARKET

Futures contracts serve several key functions in the natural gas market, including hedging, speculation, and price discovery.

1. HEDGING

Risk Management: Futures contracts are commonly used by producers, consumers, and traders to manage price risk. By locking in a price for future delivery, market participants can protect themselves against adverse price movements and stabilize their financial positions.

Production and Consumption Planning: Producers and consumers use futures contracts to plan their production and consumption strategies. Hedging with futures allows them to secure future prices and budget more effectively.

2. SPECULATION

Price Speculation: Traders and investors use futures contracts to speculate on future price movements of natural gas. By taking long or short positions, speculators aim to profit from anticipated changes in market prices.

Market Trends: Futures contracts provide insights into market expectations and trends. Speculators' activities can influence market sentiment and contribute to price movements.

3. PRICE DISCOVERY

Forward Pricing: Futures contracts help establish forward prices for natural gas, reflecting market expectations of future supply and demand conditions. These forward prices serve as benchmarks for market participants and inform pricing decisions.

Market Transparency: The trading of futures contracts on exchanges enhances market transparency by providing publicly available price information and trading volumes. This transparency helps market participants make informed decisions.

MECHANICS OF FUTURES CONTRACTS

Understanding the mechanics of futures contracts is essential for effectively trading and managing these instruments. Key aspects include:

1. CONTRACT SPECIFICATIONS

Contract Size: Futures contracts specify the quantity of natural gas to be delivered. For example, a standard futures contract may represent 10,000 million British thermal units (MMBtu) of natural gas.

Delivery Date: Futures contracts have specific delivery dates, typically occurring on a monthly basis. The delivery date is the point at which the contract expires and settlement occurs.

Price Quotation: Futures prices are quoted in terms of dollars per MMBtu. Prices fluctuate based on market conditions and are determined through trading on exchanges.

2. MARGIN REQUIREMENTS

Initial Margin: To enter a futures contract, traders are required to post an initial margin, which is a percentage of the contract's total value. This margin serves as a security deposit and ensures that parties can fulfill their contractual obligations.

Maintenance Margin: Throughout the life of the contract, traders must maintain a minimum balance, known as the maintenance margin. If the account balance falls below this level, traders are required to deposit additional funds, known as a margin call.

3. SETTLEMENT

Physical Delivery: In physical delivery contracts, the seller delivers the specified quantity of natural gas to the buyer on the contract's delivery date. Physical delivery involves logistical arrangements and transfer of ownership.

Cash Settlement: In cash-settled contracts, no physical delivery occurs. Instead, the difference between the contract price and the market price on the delivery date is settled in cash. Cash settlement simplifies the process and is common in many futures contracts.

TRADING FUTURES CONTRACTS

Futures contracts are traded on regulated exchanges, where market participants buy and sell contracts based on their trading strategies and market outlook. Key aspects of trading futures contracts include:

1. EXCHANGES AND PLATFORMS

Exchanges: Futures contracts are traded on exchanges such as the New York Mercantile Exchange (NYMEX) and the Intercontinental Exchange (ICE). These exchanges provide a platform for trading, clearing, and settling futures contracts.

Trading Platforms: Traders use electronic trading platforms to place orders, monitor prices, and manage their positions. These platforms offer real-time market data and trading tools.

2. TRADING STRATEGIES

Long and Short Positions: Traders can take long positions (buy) if they expect prices to rise or short positions (sell) if they anticipate prices will fall. Position management and timing are crucial for successful trading.

Spread Trading: Spread trading involves taking simultaneous long and short positions in different futures contracts to profit from price differentials. Common spread strategies include calendar (same commodity) spreads and intercommodity (two or more related commodity) spreads.

3. RISK MANAGEMENT

Hedging: Traders use futures contracts to hedge against price risks by offsetting potential losses in other investments or business operations. Effective hedging strategies help manage exposure and reduce risk.

Stop-Loss Orders: Stop-loss orders are used to limit potential losses by automatically closing a position when the market reaches a specified price level. These orders help manage risk and protect against significant losses.

IMPACT OF FUTURES CONTRACTS ON THE MARKET

Futures contracts have a significant impact on the natural gas market, influencing pricing, liquidity, and market behavior.

1. PRICE INFLUENCE

Price Discovery: Futures contracts contribute to price discovery by reflecting market expectations of future supply and demand conditions. Forward prices derived from futures contracts help establish benchmarks for the natural gas market.

Market Sentiment: The activities of futures traders, including speculation and hedging, can influence market sentiment and contribute to price movements. Large trading volumes and significant positions can impact market dynamics.

2. MARKET LIQUIDITY

Increased Liquidity: The trading of futures contracts enhances market liquidity by providing a mechanism for buying and selling natural gas in standardized quantities. Increased liquidity facilitates efficient trading and price discovery.

Access to Markets: Futures contracts provide market participants with access to natural gas markets and trading opportunities. This accessibility contributes to a more vibrant and competitive market.

Futures contracts are a vital tool in the natural gas market, offering mechanisms for hedging, speculation, and price discovery. By understanding the mechanics, trading strategies, and impact of futures contracts, traders and investors can effectively navigate the natural gas market and manage their exposure to price fluctuations. Futures contracts play a crucial role in shaping market dynamics, influencing pricing, and ensuring liquidity in the natural gas market.

CHAPTER 15: OPTIONS AND DERIVATIVES

Options and derivatives are sophisticated financial instruments that provide traders and investors with additional tools for managing risk, speculating on price movements, and enhancing trading strategies. In the natural gas market, these instruments play a crucial role in refining trading approaches and optimizing financial outcomes. This chapter explores the basics of options and derivatives, their applications in the natural gas market, and key considerations for using these instruments effectively.

WHAT ARE DERIVATIVES?

Derivatives are financial contracts whose value is derived from the performance of an underlying asset, such as natural gas. These contracts are used for hedging, speculation, and arbitrage, providing market participants with various strategies to manage risk and capitalize on price movements.

1. KEY TYPES OF DERIVATIVES

Derivatives are financial instruments that derive their value from an underlying asset, such as natural gas. They are commonly used in trading to manage risk, hedge against price fluctuations, and speculate on market movements. Below are the key types of derivatives frequently used in natural gas trading, along with examples to illustrate their applications.

Futures Contracts: Futures contracts are standardized agreements to buy or sell an asset, such as natural gas, at a predetermined price on a specific future date. They are traded on exchanges, making them highly liquid and transparent.

Example: A natural gas producer anticipates that gas prices may drop in the next six months due to an expected increase in supply. To protect against this potential decline, the producer enters into a futures contract to sell a specific quantity of natural gas at the current market price, locking in the price today. Even if the market price falls six months later, the producer can sell the gas at the agreed-upon price, effectively hedging against the price drop.

Options Contracts: Options contracts give the holder the right, but not the obligation, to buy or sell an underlying asset at a specified price (the strike price) before or at the contract's expiration date. Options can be used for both hedging and speculative purposes, providing flexibility in trading strategies.

Example: A natural gas trader believes that gas prices will rise in the coming months due to an anticipated cold winter. The trader purchases a call option, which gives them the right to buy natural gas at a specific price (the strike price) within the next three months. If gas prices increase as expected, the trader can exercise the option and buy gas at the lower strike price, then sell it at the higher market price, profiting from the difference. If prices don't rise, the trader can choose not to exercise the option, limiting the loss to the premium paid for the option.

Swaps: Swaps are agreements between two parties to exchange cash flows or other financial instruments based on underlying variables, such as interest rates, currency exchange rates, or commodity prices. In the natural gas market, swaps are often used to exchange fixed-price payments for floating-price payments.

Example: A utility company that buys natural gas at fluctuating market prices is concerned about potential price spikes. To manage this risk, the utility enters into a swap agreement with a financial institution. Under the swap, the utility agrees to pay a fixed price for natural gas, while the financial institution pays the floating market price. If market prices rise above the fixed price, the utility benefits by paying the lower fixed price, while the financial institution covers the higher market price. Conversely, if prices fall, the utility pays more than the market price, but this risk is mitigated by the stability provided by the swap.

Forward Contracts: Forward contracts are similar to futures contracts but are customized agreements between two parties to buy or sell an asset at a specific price on a future date. Unlike futures, forwards are not standardized or traded on exchanges, allowing for more flexibility in terms and conditions.

Example: A commercial buyer needs to secure a large quantity of natural gas for delivery in one year. Concerned about potential price increases, the buyer enters into a forward contract with a supplier to purchase the gas at a fixed price, agreed upon today, for delivery in a year. This contract allows the buyer to lock in the current price, ensuring budget certainty and protection against future price volatility. If market prices rise over the year, the buyer benefits by paying the lower, agreed-upon price.

UNDERSTANDING OPTIONS CONTRACTS

Options contracts are versatile instruments that offer a range of strategies for managing risk and speculating on price movements. There are two main types of options: call options and put options.

1. CALL OPTIONS

A call option gives the holder the right to buy the underlying asset at a specified price (the strike price) before or at the expiration date. Call options are used when an investor expects the price of the asset to rise.

Applications: Traders use call options to speculate on rising prices, hedge against potential price increases, or enhance existing positions. For example, a trader might buy call options to benefit from anticipated upward movement in natural gas prices.

2. PUT OPTIONS

A put option gives the holder the right to sell the underlying asset at a specified price (the strike price) before or at the expiration date. Put options are used when an investor expects the price of the asset to fall.

Applications: Put options are used to hedge against price declines, speculate on falling prices, or protect existing positions. For example, a natural gas producer might buy put options to safeguard against potential price drops.

3. OPTION PREMIUMS

Premiums: The cost of purchasing an option is known as the premium. The premium is influenced by various factors, including the underlying asset's price, strike price, time to expiration, and market volatility.

Valuation: Option premiums are determined by models such as the Black-Scholes model, which factors in the underlying asset's price, strike price, time value, and market conditions. Understanding these factors helps in evaluating the cost and potential profitability of options.

APPLICATIONS OF OPTIONS AND DERIVATIVES IN NATURAL GAS TRADING

Options and derivatives provide market participants with tools to manage risk, optimize trading strategies, and enhance financial outcomes. Key applications include:

1. HEDGING STRATEGIES

Price Protection: Options and derivatives are commonly used to hedge against adverse price movements. For example, natural gas producers might use futures and options to lock in prices and protect their revenue against price declines.

Risk Management: By employing various derivative instruments, market participants can manage risks associated with price volatility, interest rate changes, and other market factors. Hedging strategies help stabilize financial performance and mitigate potential losses.

2. SPECULATION

Leverage: Derivatives allow traders to take leveraged positions, amplifying their potential gains (and losses) based on price movements. Speculators use options and futures to profit from anticipated price changes in the natural gas market.

Arbitrage: Traders use derivatives to exploit price differentials between related markets or instruments. Arbitrage opportunities arise when discrepancies exist between spot prices, futures prices, and other related contracts.

3. PORTFOLIO OPTIMIZATION

Diversification: Derivatives can be used to diversify trading portfolios by incorporating various strategies and instruments. This diversification helps spread risk and enhance overall portfolio performance.

Strategic Positioning: Market participants use derivatives to adjust their positions based on market conditions and strategic goals. For example, combining options with futures can create complex strategies tailored to specific market views.

RISKS AND CONSIDERATIONS

While options and derivatives offer significant advantages, they also involve risks and considerations that market participants must address:

1. MARKET RISK

Price Fluctuations: Derivatives are subject to price fluctuations and market volatility. Traders must be prepared for potential losses and manage their exposure accordingly.

Leverage Risk: Leverage amplifies both potential gains and losses. Traders should carefully consider their risk tolerance and employ appropriate risk management strategies.

2. COMPLEXITY AND COSTS

Complexity: Options and derivatives can be complex financial instruments with various factors influencing their value. Traders must understand the intricacies of these instruments to use them effectively.

Transaction Costs: Trading options and derivatives may involve transaction costs, including commissions, fees, and bid-ask spreads. These costs can impact the overall profitability of trading strategies.

3. REGULATORY AND COMPLIANCE ISSUES

Regulation: Derivatives markets are subject to regulatory oversight to ensure market integrity and protect participants. Traders should stay informed about relevant regulations and comply with legal requirements.

Reporting Requirements: Some derivatives transactions may involve reporting requirements and transparency obligations. Participants should be aware of their reporting obligations and ensure compliance.

Options and derivatives are powerful tools in the natural gas market, offering opportunities for hedging, speculation, and portfolio optimization. By understanding the mechanics, applications, and risks associated with these instruments, traders and investors can enhance their trading strategies and manage their market exposure more effectively. Options and derivatives play a critical role in shaping market dynamics, providing flexibility, and optimizing financial outcomes in the natural gas market.

CHAPTER 16: UNDERSTANDING CFDS

Contracts for Difference (CFDs) are financial instruments that allow traders and investors to speculate on price movements of various assets, including natural gas, without owning the underlying asset. CFDs provide a flexible and leveraged way to trade on price changes, offering opportunities for both hedging and speculation. This chapter explores the fundamentals of CFDs, their mechanics, applications, and key considerations for trading these instruments in the natural gas market.

WHAT ARE CFDS?

A Contract for Difference (CFD) is a financial agreement between two parties to exchange the difference in the value of an asset from the time the contract is opened to when it is closed. CFDs are derivative instruments that enable traders to profit from price movements without owning the underlying asset.

Example: Imagine you're interested in trading natural gas but don't want to own any physical natural gas. You believe the price of natural gas will rise, so you decide to open a CFD. At the time you enter the contract, natural gas is priced at $2.50 per unit.

A week later, the price of natural gas has increased to $3.00 per unit. If you close the CFD at this point, the difference in price is $0.50 per unit. Since you don't actually own the gas, the CFD provider pays you the $0.50 per unit profit (multiplied by however many units you traded).

On the flip side, if the price had dropped to $2.00 per unit, you would owe the provider $0.50 per unit instead, resulting in a loss. CFDs give you the flexibility to trade on price movements, both up and down, without the need to purchase the actual asset.

KEY CHARACTERISTICS OF CFDS

Leverage: CFDs are traded on margin, meaning traders only need to deposit a fraction of the total trade value. Leverage allows traders to control a larger position with a smaller amount of capital, amplifying both potential gains and losses.

No Ownership: Unlike traditional asset purchases, CFDs do not involve owning the underlying asset. Traders are speculating on price movements rather than buying or selling the actual asset.

Long and Short Positions: CFDs allow traders to take both long (buy) and short (sell) positions. This flexibility enables traders to profit from both rising and falling markets.

HOW CFDS WORK

Understanding the mechanics of CFDs is essential for effective trading. Key aspects include:

1. OPENING A CFD POSITION

Trade Execution: To open a CFD position, a trader selects the asset they wish to trade (e.g., natural gas) and chooses whether to go long or short. The trader then specifies the trade size and enters the position.

Leverage and Margin: The required margin is determined by the leverage offered by the broker. For example, a 10% margin requirement means the trader needs to deposit 10% of the total position value to open the trade.

2. PROFIT AND LOSS CALCULATION

Price Movements: The profit or loss in a CFD trade is calculated based on the difference between the entry price and the exit price of the position. For a long position, profit occurs if the price rises; for a short position, profit occurs if the price falls.

Example Calculation: If a trader buys a CFD on natural gas at $3.00 per MMBtu and sells it at $3.20 per MMBtu, the profit is the difference between the two prices multiplied by the trade size. Conversely, if the price falls, the trader incurs a loss.

3. CLOSING A CFD POSITION

Exit Strategy: To close a CFD position, the trader executes an opposite trade to the initial position. For a long position, this means selling the CFD; for a short position, it means buying the CFD.

Settlement: The difference between the opening and closing prices determines the final profit or loss. The position is settled in cash, reflecting the net gain or loss.

APPLICATIONS OF CFDS IN NATURAL GAS TRADING

CFDs offer various applications for trading and managing natural gas positions. Key uses include:

1. SPECULATION

Market Opportunities: Traders use CFDs to speculate on price movements of natural gas based on market analysis and forecasts. CFDs allow traders to take advantage of short-term price changes and profit from market fluctuations.

Leverage: The leverage offered by CFDs enables traders to amplify their potential returns on successful trades. However, leverage also increases the risk of significant losses if the market moves against the position.

2. HEDGING

Risk Management: CFDs can be used to hedge existing positions or portfolios against adverse price movements. For example, a trader holding a long position in natural gas futures might use CFDs to hedge against potential price declines.

Flexibility: CFDs provide a flexible and cost-effective way to hedge positions without requiring physical delivery of the underlying asset. This flexibility makes CFDs a popular choice for managing risk.

3. PORTFOLIO DIVERSIFICATION

Diversification: Traders use CFDs to diversify their portfolios by gaining exposure to different assets and markets. CFDs on natural gas can be part of a broader trading strategy that includes other commodities, equities, or currencies.

Tactical Positioning: CFDs enable traders to adjust their portfolio positions based on market conditions and strategic goals. This adaptability helps optimize portfolio performance and manage exposure.

RISKS AND CONSIDERATIONS

Trading CFDs involves specific risks and considerations that traders should be aware of:

1. MARKET RISK

Price Volatility: CFDs are subject to market volatility and price fluctuations. Traders must be prepared for rapid changes in market conditions that can impact their positions and financial outcomes.

Leverage Risk: While leverage can amplify gains, it also magnifies losses. Traders should use leverage cautiously and ensure they have a clear risk management strategy in place.

2. COSTS AND FEES

Spread and Commissions: CFD trading involves costs such as the bid-ask spread and commissions. These costs can affect the overall profitability of trades and should be considered when evaluating trading strategies.

Overnight Financing: Holding CFD positions overnight may incur financing costs or interest charges. Traders should be aware of these costs and factor them into their trading decisions.

3. REGULATORY CONSIDERATIONS

Regulation: CFD trading is subject to regulatory oversight in various jurisdictions. Traders should ensure they are trading with regulated brokers and comply with relevant regulations and requirements.

Broker Selection: Choosing a reputable and regulated CFD broker is crucial for ensuring fair trading conditions and protecting investor interests. Traders should conduct thorough research before selecting a broker.

Contracts for Difference (CFDs) offer a flexible and leveraged approach to trading natural gas and other assets, providing opportunities for speculation, hedging, and portfolio diversification. By understanding the mechanics, applications, and risks of CFDs, traders can effectively navigate the natural gas market and implement strategies to manage their risk and optimize their trading outcomes. CFDs play a significant role in modern trading, offering tools to capitalize on price movements and manage financial exposure.

PART 5: TECHNICAL ANALYSIS FOR NATURAL GAS TRADING

CHAPTER 17: CHART PATTERNS AND TRENDS

Chart patterns and trends are essential tools in technical analysis, helping traders make informed decisions based on historical price data and market behavior. By recognizing and understanding these patterns, traders can better predict potential price movements and develop effective trading strategies. This chapter explores the basics of chart patterns and trends, their significance in natural gas trading, and how to apply them to enhance trading performance.

INTRODUCTION TO CHART PATTERNS AND TRENDS

Chart patterns are visual representations of price movements in a market, typically displayed on a price chart. These patterns can signal potential future price movements and help traders make predictions about market direction. Trends, on the other hand, refer to the general direction in which the price of an asset is moving over a certain period.

1. TYPES OF CHARTS

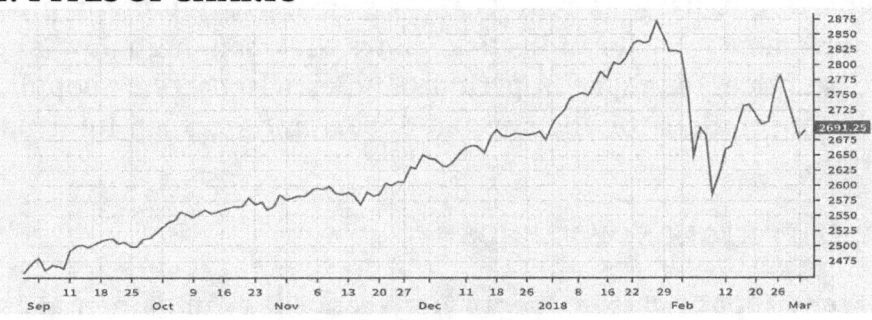

Line Chart: investopedia.com

Line Charts: Line charts connect a series of closing prices over a specific period. They provide a clear overview of the asset's price movement but offer less detail than other chart types.

Bar Chart: forextraininggroup.com

Bar Charts: Bar charts display the open, high, low, and close prices for each period. This chart type provides more information than a line chart and helps traders analyze price ranges and market sentiment.

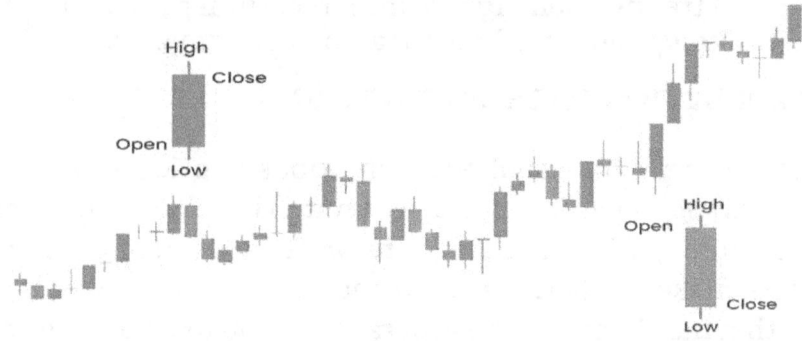

Candlestick charts: moneysukh.com

Candlestick Charts: Candlestick charts are similar to bar charts but use different visual elements to represent price movements. Each candlestick shows the open, high, low, and close prices for a specific period. Candlestick charts are popular among traders for their visual appeal and detailed information.

2. IMPORTANCE OF TRENDS

Trend Identification: Identifying trends is a fundamental aspect of technical analysis. Trends help traders determine the overall direction of the market and make informed trading decisions.

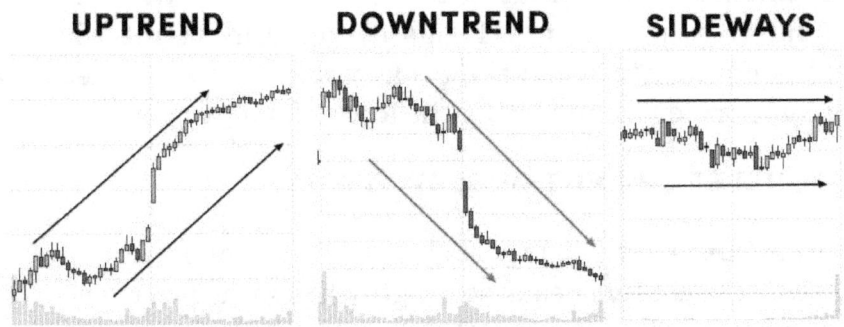

Trend Trading: danielsash.medium.com

Types of Trends: Trends can be classified into three types: uptrends, downtrends, and sideways trends. Uptrends are characterized by higher highs and higher lows, downtrends by lower highs and lower lows, and sideways trends by relatively stable prices.

COMMON CHART PATTERNS

Chart patterns are formed by the price movements of an asset over time and can provide insights into potential future price actions. Some common chart patterns include:

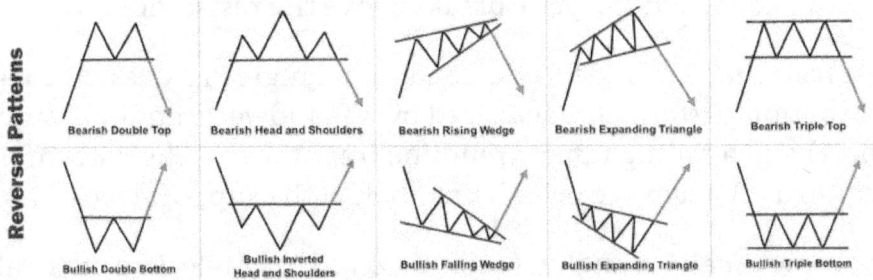

Chart Patterns (Reversal): changelly.com

1. HEAD AND SHOULDERS

The head and shoulders pattern is a reversal pattern that signals a potential trend change from bullish to bearish. It consists of three peaks: the left shoulder, the head, and the right shoulder.

Identification: The head is the highest peak, with the two shoulders being lower and roughly equal in height. The pattern is confirmed when the price breaks below the neckline, the support level connecting the lows of the two shoulders.

2. DOUBLE TOP AND DOUBLE BOTTOM

Double Top: A double top is a bearish reversal pattern formed by two consecutive peaks at roughly the same price level. The pattern is confirmed when the price breaks below the support level between the two peaks.

Double Bottom: A double bottom is a bullish reversal pattern formed by two consecutive lows at roughly the same price level. The pattern is confirmed when the price breaks above the resistance level between the two lows.

3. TRIANGLES

Ascending Triangle: An ascending triangle is a bullish continuation pattern characterized by a flat upper trendline (resistance) and a rising lower trendline (support). The pattern is confirmed when the price breaks above the resistance level.

Descending Triangle: A descending triangle is a bearish continuation pattern characterized by a flat lower trendline (support) and a falling upper trendline (resistance). The pattern is confirmed when the price breaks below the support level.

Symmetrical Triangle: A symmetrical triangle is a neutral pattern that can signal a continuation or reversal of the existing trend. It is formed by converging upper and lower trendlines. The pattern is confirmed when the price breaks out in either direction.

4. FLAGS AND PENNANTS

Flags: Flags are continuation patterns that resemble a small rectangle or parallelogram sloping against the prevailing trend. They indicate a brief pause in the trend before the price continues in the same direction.

Pennants: Pennants are similar to flags but have a triangular shape. They also represent a brief consolidation period before the price resumes its trend.

APPLYING CHART PATTERNS AND TRENDS IN NATURAL GAS TRADING

Chart patterns and trends are valuable tools for traders in the natural gas market. By applying these techniques, traders can enhance their trading strategies and improve their decision-making process.

1. TREND-FOLLOWING STRATEGIES

Moving Averages: Moving averages are commonly used to identify trends and generate trading signals. Traders use moving averages to smooth out price data and identify the direction of the trend. For example, a trader might use a moving average crossover strategy, buying when the short-term moving average crosses above the long-term moving average and selling when it crosses below.

Trendlines: Trendlines are drawn on price charts to identify the direction of the trend and potential support and resistance levels. Traders use trendlines to determine entry and exit points for their trades.

2. REVERSAL STRATEGIES

Pattern Recognition: Traders use chart patterns such as head and shoulders, double tops, and double bottoms to identify potential trend reversals. By recognizing these patterns, traders can anticipate changes in market direction and adjust their positions accordingly.

Oscillators: Oscillators such as the Relative Strength Index (RSI) and the Moving Average Convergence Divergence (MACD) are used to identify overbought and oversold conditions in the market. These indicators can help traders identify potential reversal points and make informed trading decisions.

3. BREAKOUT STRATEGIES

Triangle Patterns: Traders use triangle patterns such as ascending, descending, and symmetrical triangles to identify potential breakouts. By analyzing the volume and price action during the formation of these patterns, traders can anticipate breakouts and take advantage of potential price movements.

Flags and Pennants: Flags and pennants are used to identify potential continuation patterns. Traders monitor these patterns for breakout signals and enter trades in the direction of the prevailing trend.

RISKS AND CONSIDERATIONS

While chart patterns and trends are valuable tools, they also involve certain risks and considerations that traders should be aware of:

1. FALSE SIGNALS

Market Noise: Chart patterns and trends can sometimes generate false signals due to market noise and volatility. Traders should use additional indicators and analysis techniques to confirm signals and reduce the risk of false trades.

Pattern Recognition: Identifying chart patterns and trends requires skill and experience. Traders should practice recognizing patterns and validating signals before incorporating them into their trading strategies.

2. MARKET CONDITIONS

Changing Market Conditions: Market conditions can change rapidly, affecting the reliability of chart patterns and trends. Traders should be prepared to adapt their strategies based on evolving market dynamics.

Limitations of Technical Analysis: While chart patterns and trends are useful tools, they are not foolproof. Traders should use a combination of technical and fundamental analysis to make informed trading decisions.

Chart patterns and trends are essential components of technical analysis, providing traders with valuable insights into market behavior and potential price movements. By understanding and applying these tools, traders can enhance their trading strategies, improve their decision-making process, and increase their chances of success in the natural gas market. However, it is essential to recognize the limitations and risks associated with chart patterns and trends and to use them in conjunction with other analysis techniques for optimal results.

CHAPTER 18: MOVING AVERAGES AND INDICATORS

Technical indicators are mathematical calculations used to analyze historical price data and predict future price movements in the natural gas market. Moving averages and various technical indicators are key tools in technical analysis that help traders identify trends, generate signals, and make informed trading decisions. This chapter explores the basics of moving averages and other popular technical indicators, their applications in natural gas trading, and how traders can integrate them into their trading strategies.

INTRODUCTION TO MOVING AVERAGES

Moving averages (MAs) are among the most widely used technical indicators in trading. They smooth out price data to create a single flowing line that represents the average price of an asset over a specific period. By using moving averages, traders can identify trends and potential reversal points in the market.

1. TYPES OF MOVING AVERAGES

Simple Moving Average (SMA): The simple moving average is calculated by adding the closing prices of an asset over a specific period and dividing the total by the number of periods. The SMA is a basic yet effective tool for identifying trends.

CHAPTER 18: MOVING AVERAGES AND INDICATORS | 115

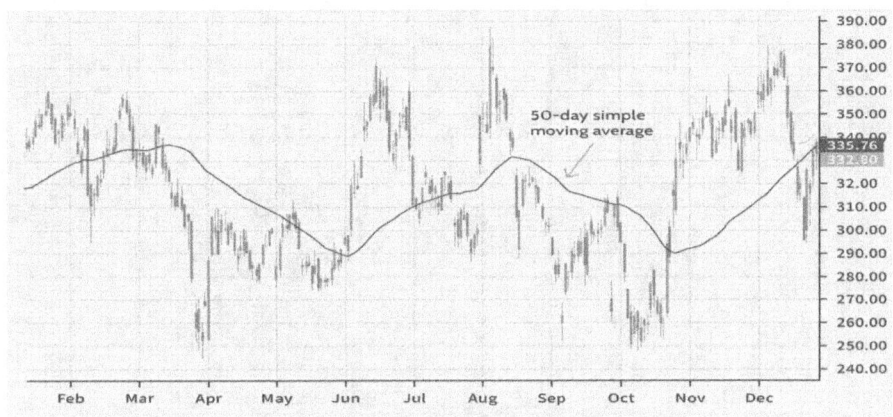

Simple Moving Average (SMA): investopedia.com

Exponential Moving Average (EMA): The exponential moving average gives more weight to recent price data, making it more responsive to current market conditions. The EMA is particularly useful for traders looking to identify short-term trends and potential entry and exit points.

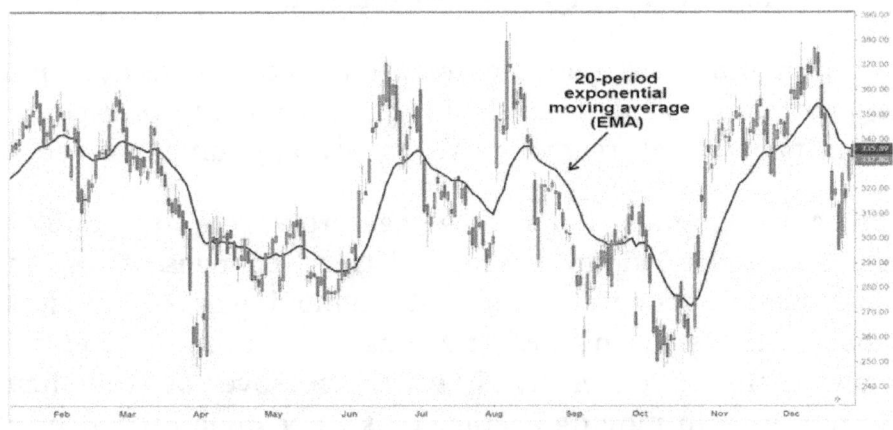

Exponential Moving Average (SMA): investopedia.com

Weighted Moving Average (WMA): The weighted moving average assigns different weights to each data point in the calculation, with more recent prices given higher weights. The WMA is similar to the EMA but uses a different weighting scheme.

Weighted Moving Average (SMA): investopedia.com

2. APPLICATIONS OF MOVING AVERAGES IN TRADING

Trend Identification: Moving averages are primarily used to identify the direction of the trend. When the price is above the moving average, it indicates an uptrend, while a price below the moving average suggests a downtrend.

Support and Resistance: Moving averages can act as dynamic support and resistance levels. Traders use moving averages to identify potential areas where the price may bounce or reverse.

Crossover Signals: Moving average crossovers are popular signals used to identify potential trend changes. A bullish crossover occurs when a shorter-term moving average crosses above a longer-term moving average, indicating a potential upward trend. Conversely, a bearish crossover occurs when a shorter-term moving average crosses below a longer-term moving average, indicating a potential downward trend.

COMMON TECHNICAL INDICATORS

In addition to moving averages, traders use a variety of technical indicators to analyze market conditions and generate trading signals. Some of the most commonly used technical indicators include:

1. RELATIVE STRENGTH INDEX (RSI)

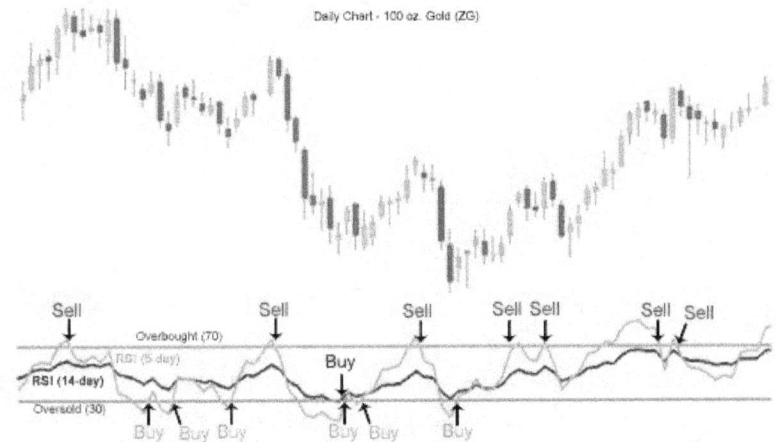

Relative Strength Index (RSI) bottom chart. commodity.com

The Relative Strength Index (RSI) is a momentum oscillator that measures the speed and change of price movements. It oscillates between 0 and 100, with readings above 70 indicating overbought conditions and readings below 30 indicating oversold conditions.

Applications: Traders use the RSI to identify potential reversal points and confirm trend strength. A divergence between the RSI and the price can signal a potential trend reversal.

2. MOVING AVERAGE CONVERGENCE DIVERGENCE (MACD)

The MACD (Moving Average Convergence Divergence) is a trend-following momentum indicator that highlights the relationship between two moving averages of an asset's price. The MACD line is calculated by subtracting the 26-period EMA from the 12-period EMA, and a 9-period EMA is plotted on top as the signal line.

The MACD histogram visualizes the difference between the MACD line and the signal line, providing insight into trend strength. When the MACD line crosses above the signal line, it may signal a potential buying opportunity; conversely, when it crosses below, it could indicate a potential selling opportunity.

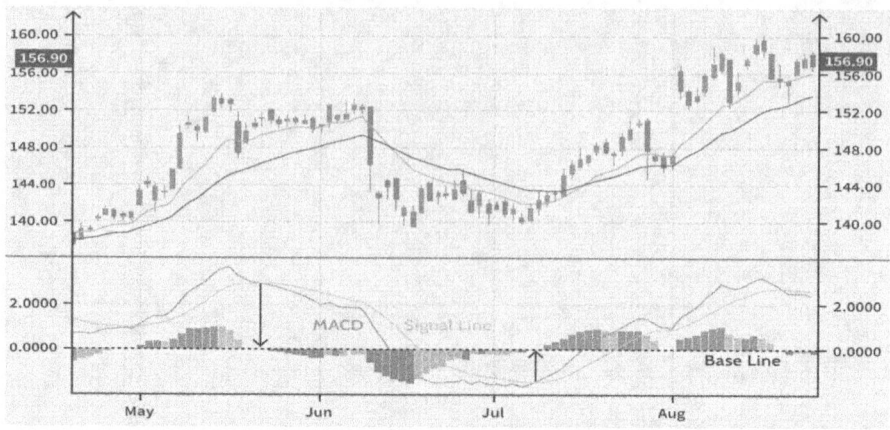

Moving Average Convergence Divergence (MACD): investopedia.com

Applications: Traders use the MACD to identify potential trend changes and generate trading signals. A bullish signal occurs when the MACD line crosses above the signal line, while a bearish signal occurs when the MACD line crosses below the signal line.

3. BOLLINGER BANDS

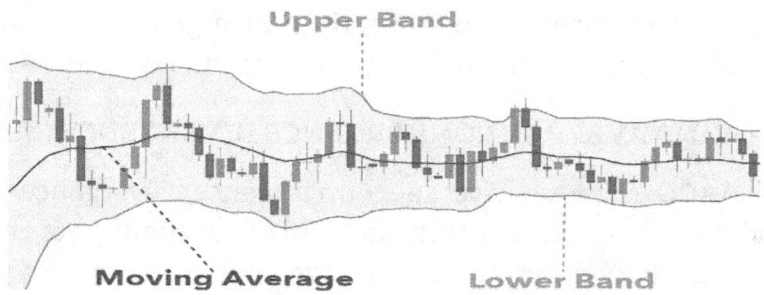

Bollinger Bands : dailyfx.com

Bollinger Bands consist of a moving average and two standard deviation lines plotted above and below the moving average. The bands expand and contract based on market volatility.

Applications: Traders use Bollinger Bands to identify potential breakouts and measure market volatility. When the price touches or moves outside the bands, it may indicate a potential reversal or continuation of the trend.

4. STOCHASTIC OSCILLATOR

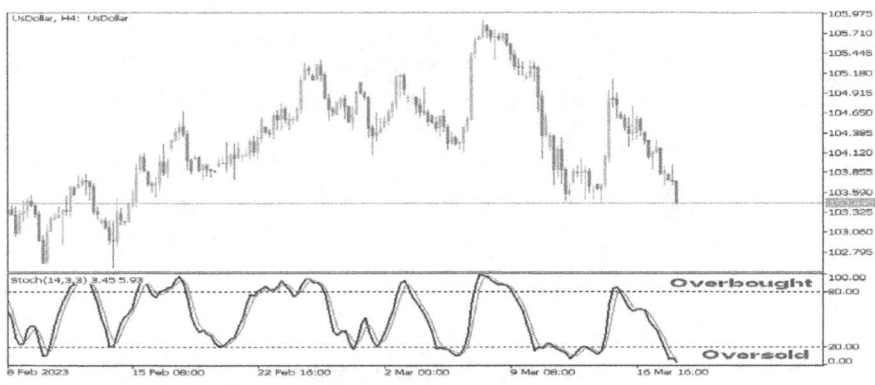

Stochastic Oscillator : fbs.com

The Stochastic Oscillator is a momentum indicator that compares the closing price of an asset to its price range over a specific period. It oscillates between 0 and 100, with readings above 80 indicating overbought conditions and readings below 20 indicating oversold conditions.

Applications: Traders use the Stochastic Oscillator to identify potential reversal points and confirm trend strength. Like the RSI, divergences between the Stochastic Oscillator and the price can signal potential trend reversals.

INTEGRATING MOVING AVERAGES AND INDICATORS INTO TRADING STRATEGIES

Traders can integrate moving averages and technical indicators into their trading strategies to enhance their analysis and decision-making process. Key approaches include:

1. TREND-FOLLOWING STRATEGIES

Moving Average Crossovers: Traders use moving average crossovers to identify potential trend changes and generate trading signals.

Moving Average Crossovers : dailyfx.com

For example, a trader might enter a long position when the 50-day EMA crosses above the 200-day EMA and exit the position when the 50-day EMA crosses below the 200-day EMA.

Confirmation with Indicators: Traders use technical indicators such as the MACD and RSI to confirm trend direction and strength. For example, a trader might look for a bullish MACD crossover and an RSI reading above 50 to confirm an uptrend.

2. REVERSAL STRATEGIES

Divergence Analysis

Divergence occurs when the price of an asset moves in the opposite direction of a technical indicator, such as an oscillator, or conflicts with other data.

This divergence signals that the current price trend might be losing strength and could potentially reverse direction.

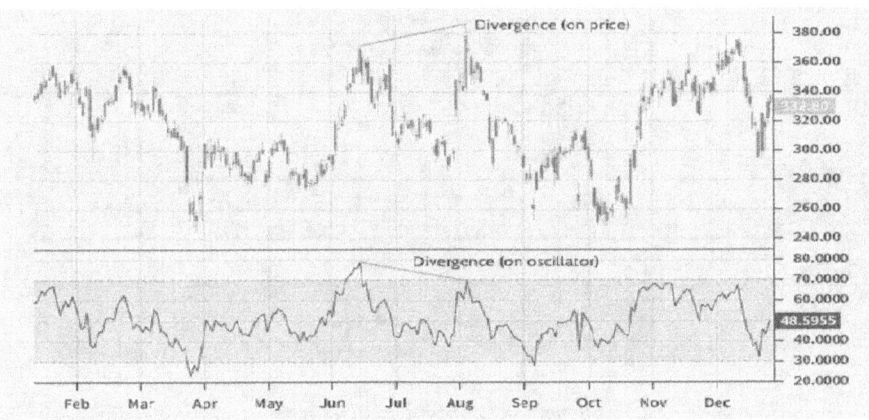

Divergence Analysis : investopedia.com

There are two types of divergence:

Positive Divergence: This suggests that the price of the asset might be set to move higher. It occurs when the price is falling or moving sideways, but the technical indicator is rising, indicating underlying strength in the asset.

Negative Divergence: This warns that the price could move lower. It happens when the price is rising or holding steady, but the technical indicator is falling, hinting at underlying weakness in the asset.

Traders use divergence analysis with indicators such as the RSI and Stochastic Oscillator to identify potential reversal points. For example, a trader might look for a bearish divergence between the RSI and the price to signal a potential trend reversal.

Support and Resistance Levels

Support and Resistance Levels are key price points where buying or selling pressure tends to concentrate, often acting as psychological barriers that influence the direction of an asset's price movement.

Support and resistance: dailyfx.com

Support Level: This is a price point where a downward trend is likely to pause or reverse due to a surge in demand. As the price nears the support level, buyers are more inclined to step in, preventing the price from falling further. It serves as a "floor" that the asset's price frequently touches but struggles to fall below for a certain period.

Resistance Level: This is a price point where an upward trend is expected to stall or reverse due to increased selling pressure. As the price approaches the resistance level, sellers are more likely to take action, preventing the price from rising further. It acts as a "ceiling" that the asset's price often reaches but fails to break above for a certain period.

3. BREAKOUT STRATEGIES

Volatility Breakouts:forextraininggroup.com

Volatility Breakouts: Traders use Bollinger Bands to identify potential breakouts based on market volatility. For example, a trader might enter a long position when the price breaks above the upper Bollinger Band and exit the position when the price returns to the middle band.

Indicator Confirmation: Traders use indicators such as the MACD and Stochastic Oscillator to confirm breakout signals. For example, a trader might look for a bullish MACD crossover and a Stochastic Oscillator reading above 50 to confirm a breakout.

RISKS AND CONSIDERATIONS

While moving averages and technical indicators are valuable tools, they also involve certain risks and considerations that traders should be aware of:

1. LAGGING NATURE OF INDICATORS

Delayed Signals: Moving averages and other technical indicators are based on historical price data and may generate delayed signals. Traders should be aware of the lagging nature of these indicators and use them in conjunction with other analysis techniques.

False Signals: Indicators can generate false signals due to market noise and volatility. Traders should use additional indicators and analysis techniques to confirm signals and reduce the risk of false trades.

2. MARKET CONDITIONS

Changing Market Conditions: Market conditions can change rapidly, affecting the reliability of moving averages and technical indicators. Traders should be prepared to adapt their strategies based on evolving market dynamics.

Limitations of Technical Analysis: While moving averages and technical indicators are useful tools, they are not foolproof. Traders should use a combination of technical and fundamental analysis to make informed trading decisions.

Moving averages and technical indicators are essential components of technical analysis, providing traders with valuable insights into market behavior and potential price movements. By understanding and applying these tools, traders can enhance their trading strategies, improve their decision-making process, and increase their chances of success in the natural gas market. However, it is essential to recognize the limitations and risks associated with moving averages and technical indicators and to use them in conjunction with other analysis techniques for optimal results.

CHAPTER 19: VOLUME ANALYSIS

Volume analysis is a critical aspect of technical analysis, offering traders valuable insights into the strength of price movements and the underlying dynamics of the natural gas market. By studying volume data, traders can assess market activity, confirm trends, and identify potential trading opportunities. This chapter delves into the fundamentals of volume analysis, its applications in natural gas trading, and how traders can incorporate volume indicators into their trading strategies.

INTRODUCTION TO VOLUME ANALYSIS

Volume represents the total number of contracts or units traded in a given period and is a key indicator of market activity. By analyzing volume data, traders can gauge the level of interest and participation in the market, helping them make informed trading decisions.

1. IMPORTANCE OF VOLUME IN TRADING

Confirmation of Trends: Volume is used to confirm the strength of trends. A strong trend is typically accompanied by high volume, while a weak trend may be characterized by low volume. By analyzing volume data, traders can assess the validity of price movements and avoid false signals.

Identification of Reversals: Sudden spikes or declines in volume can signal potential trend reversals. For example, a sharp increase in volume during a downtrend may indicate a shift in market sentiment and the start of a new uptrend.

Assessment of Market Strength: Volume provides insights

into the strength of market moves. High volume indicates strong participation and interest, while low volume suggests a lack of conviction among traders.

2. TYPES OF VOLUME INDICATORS

Several volume indicators are used in technical analysis to interpret volume data and generate trading signals. Some of the most commonly used volume indicators include:

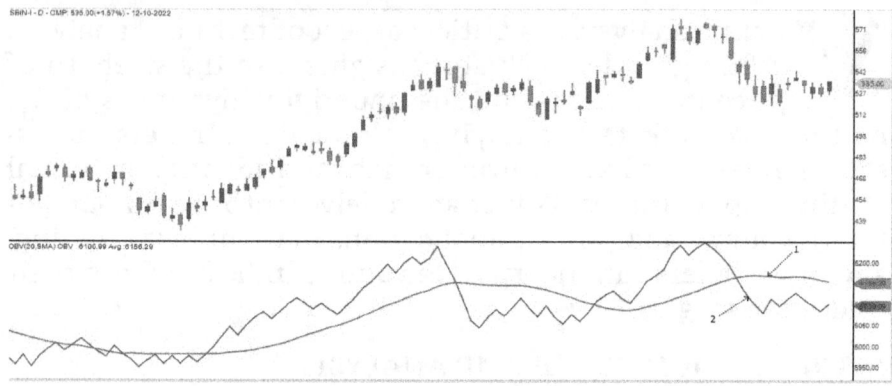

On-Balance Volume (OBV) Indicator: definedgesecurities.com

On-Balance Volume (OBV): The OBV indicator measures buying and selling pressure by adding volume on up days and subtracting volume on down days. It helps traders identify trends and confirm price movements.

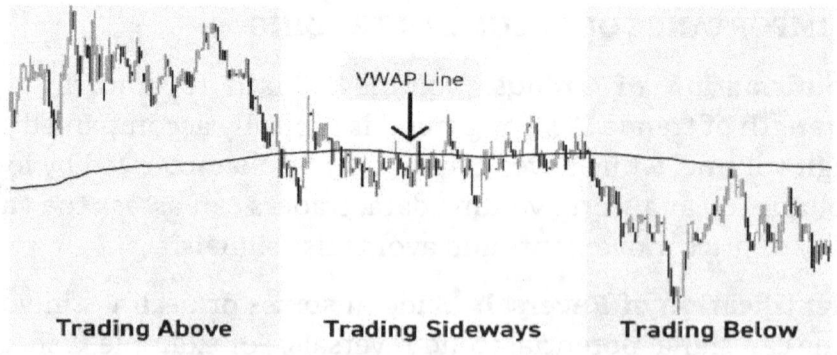

Volume Weighted Average Price (VWAP) Indicator: centerpointsecurities.com

Volume Weighted Average Price (VWAP): The VWAP indicator calculates the average price of an asset weighted by volume. It provides insights into the average price at which the asset was traded during a specific period and is commonly used by institutional traders.

Accumulation/Distribution Line (A/D Line): investopedia.com

Accumulation/Distribution Line (A/D Line): The A/D Line is a cumulative volume indicator that measures the flow of money into and out of an asset. It helps traders identify trends and potential reversals by analyzing the relationship between price and volume.

APPLICATIONS OF VOLUME ANALYSIS IN NATURAL GAS TRADING

Volume analysis is a valuable tool for traders in the natural gas market, offering insights into market behavior and potential trading opportunities. Some key applications of volume analysis in natural gas trading include:

1. TREND CONFIRMATION

Volume and Price Trends: Traders use volume data to confirm the strength of price trends. For example, an uptrend accompanied by increasing volume suggests strong buying pressure and a continuation of the trend. Conversely, an uptrend with declining volume may indicate weakening momentum and a potential reversal.

Divergences: Divergences between price and volume can signal potential trend reversals. For example, a bullish divergence occurs when the price makes lower lows, but the volume indicator makes higher lows, indicating a potential shift in market sentiment.

2. BREAKOUT AND BREAKDOWN SIGNALS

Volume Spikes: Sudden spikes in volume can indicate potential breakouts or breakdowns. Traders monitor volume spikes to identify significant market moves and capitalize on trading opportunities.

Support and Resistance Levels: Volume data can help traders identify key support and resistance levels. High volume at a support level indicates strong buying interest, while high volume at a resistance level suggests strong selling pressure.

3. REVERSAL PATTERNS

Volume Climax: A volume climax occurs when volume reaches unusually high levels, signaling a potential reversal. Traders use volume climax patterns to identify exhaustion points and anticipate trend changes.

Volume Gaps: Volume gaps, characterized by a significant change in volume between two periods, can signal potential reversals. Traders analyze volume gaps to assess market sentiment and identify potential entry and exit points.

INCORPORATING VOLUME INDICATORS INTO TRADING STRATEGIES

Traders can incorporate volume indicators into their trading strategies to enhance their analysis and decision-making process. Key approaches include:

1. TREND-FOLLOWING STRATEGIES

OBV and Price Trends: Traders use the OBV indicator to confirm price trends and generate trading signals. For example, a trader might enter a long position when the OBV line is rising and the price is in an uptrend, and exit the position when the OBV line starts to decline.

VWAP and Moving Averages: Traders use the VWAP indicator in conjunction with moving averages to identify potential entry and exit points. For example, a trader might enter a long position when the price is above the VWAP and the moving average, and exit the position when the price falls below the VWAP.

2. REVERSAL STRATEGIES

A/D Line and Divergences: Traders use the A/D Line to identify divergences between price and volume. For example, a trader might enter a long position when the price makes lower lows, but the A/D Line makes higher lows, indicating a potential reversal.

Volume Climax and Exhaustion Points: Traders use volume climax patterns to identify potential exhaustion points and anticipate trend changes. For example, a trader might exit a long position when the volume reaches unusually high levels, signaling a potential reversal.

3. BREAKOUT STRATEGIES

Volume Spikes and Breakout Levels: Traders use volume spikes to identify potential breakouts and capitalize on trading opportunities. For example, a trader might enter a long position when the price breaks above a resistance level with a significant increase in volume, indicating strong buying pressure.

Volume Gaps and Market Sentiment: Traders use volume gaps to assess market sentiment and identify potential entry and exit points. For example, a trader might enter a long position when a volume gap indicates strong buying interest and a potential trend reversal.

RISKS AND CONSIDERATIONS

While volume analysis is a valuable tool, it also involves certain risks and considerations that traders should be aware of:

1. FALSE SIGNALS

Market Noise: Volume data can be affected by market noise and volatility, leading to false signals. Traders should use additional indicators and analysis techniques to confirm signals and reduce the risk of false trades.

Lagging Nature of Indicators: Volume indicators are based on historical data and may generate delayed signals. Traders should be aware of the lagging nature of these indicators and use them in conjunction with other analysis techniques.

2. MARKET CONDITIONS

Changing Market Conditions: Market conditions can change rapidly, affecting the reliability of volume data and indicators. Traders should be prepared to adapt their strategies based on evolving market dynamics.

Limitations of Technical Analysis: While volume analysis is a useful tool, it is not foolproof. Traders should use a combination of technical and fundamental analysis to make informed trading decisions.

Volume analysis is a critical component of technical analysis, providing traders with valuable insights into market behavior and potential price movements. By understanding and applying volume indicators, traders can enhance their trading strategies, improve their decision-making process, and increase their chances of success in the natural gas market.

However, it is essential to recognize the limitations and risks associated with volume analysis and to use it in conjunction with other analysis techniques for optimal results.

CHAPTER 20: USING TECHNICAL TOOLS IN MARKET DECISION-MAKING

Technical tools play a crucial role in helping traders make informed decisions in the natural gas market. By combining various technical tools, traders can enhance their analysis, identify trading opportunities, and manage risk effectively. This chapter explores the practical application of technical tools in market decision-making and provides insights into how traders can integrate these tools into their trading strategies.

OVERVIEW OF TECHNICAL TOOLS

Technical tools are mathematical and statistical calculations applied to price and volume data to identify patterns, trends, and potential trading opportunities. The most common technical tools include moving averages, trend lines, oscillators, volume indicators, and chart patterns. Each of these tools provides unique insights into market behavior and can be used to enhance the decision-making process.

1. TYPES OF TECHNICAL TOOLS

Trend Tools: These tools help traders identify the direction of the trend and potential reversal points. Examples include moving averages, trend lines, and channels.

Momentum Tools: These tools measure the speed and

strength of price movements. Examples include the Relative Strength Index (RSI), Moving Average Convergence Divergence (MACD), and Stochastic Oscillator.

Volume Tools: These tools analyze trading volume to assess market activity and confirm price movements. Examples include On-Balance Volume (OBV), Volume Weighted Average Price (VWAP), and the Accumulation/Distribution Line (A/D Line).

Volatility Tools: These tools measure market volatility and help traders identify potential breakouts and breakdowns. Examples include Bollinger Bands, Average True Range (ATR), and Keltner Channels.

Pattern Tools: These tools identify specific patterns in price data that signal potential trading opportunities. Examples include candlestick patterns, chart patterns, and Fibonacci retracements.

INTEGRATING TECHNICAL TOOLS INTO TRADING STRATEGIES

To effectively use technical tools in market decision-making, traders must integrate them into their trading strategies. This integration involves combining multiple tools, using them in conjunction with fundamental analysis, and developing a systematic approach to trading.

1. COMBINING MULTIPLE TOOLS

Trend and Momentum: Traders often combine trend tools and momentum tools to confirm trend direction and strength. For example, a trader might use moving averages to identify the trend and the MACD to assess momentum and generate trading signals.

Volume and Volatility: Traders use volume tools and volatility tools to assess market activity and identify potential breakouts. For example, a trader might use the OBV indicator to confirm price movements and Bollinger Bands to identify potential breakout points.

Pattern and Support/Resistance: Traders use pattern tools and support/resistance levels to identify potential entry and exit points. For example, a trader might use a candlestick pattern to identify a reversal and a trend line to determine a support level for entry.

2. USING TECHNICAL TOOLS WITH FUNDAMENTAL ANALYSIS

Fundamental Confirmation: Traders use technical tools to confirm fundamental analysis and assess market sentiment. For example, a trader might use a moving average crossover to confirm a bullish outlook based on supply and demand analysis.

Timing Entry and Exit: Technical tools help traders time their entry and exit points based on fundamental analysis. For example, a trader might use the RSI to identify overbought or oversold conditions and enter a trade based on a fundamental view of supply and demand.

3. DEVELOPING A SYSTEMATIC APPROACH

Trading Plan: Traders develop a trading plan that outlines their strategy, risk management, and use of technical tools. A systematic approach helps traders stay disciplined and make consistent decisions based on their analysis.

Backtesting and Optimization: Traders use backtesting to evaluate the effectiveness of their strategies and optimize their use of technical tools. By analyzing historical data, traders can refine their strategies and improve their performance.

CASE STUDIES: APPLYING TECHNICAL TOOLS IN NATURAL GAS TRADING

To illustrate the practical application of technical tools in natural gas trading, this section presents case studies of real-world scenarios where traders used technical analysis to make market decisions.

CASE STUDY 1: TREND-FOLLOWING STRATEGY WITH MOVING AVERAGES

In this case study, a trader uses moving averages to identify and follow a long-term uptrend in the natural gas market. The trader enters a short position when the 50-day EMA crosses below the 200-day EMA and exits the position when the 50-day EMA crosses above the 200-day EMA. The trader also uses the RSI to confirm the trend and assess overbought or oversold conditions.

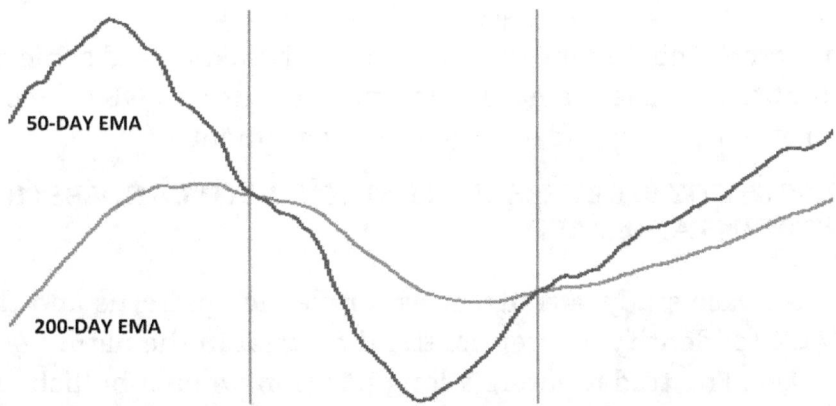

50-day EMA and 200-day EMA Strategy: investopedia.com

Outcome: The trader successfully captures a significant portion of the uptrend, using the moving average crossover as a signal to enter and exit the trade.

CASE STUDY 2: BREAKOUT STRATEGY WITH BOLLINGER

BANDS AND OBV

In this case study, a trader uses Bollinger Bands and the OBV indicator to identify a potential breakout in the natural gas market. The trader enters a long position when the price breaks above the upper Bollinger Band with a significant increase in volume, as indicated by the OBV. The trader sets a stop loss below the middle band to manage risk.

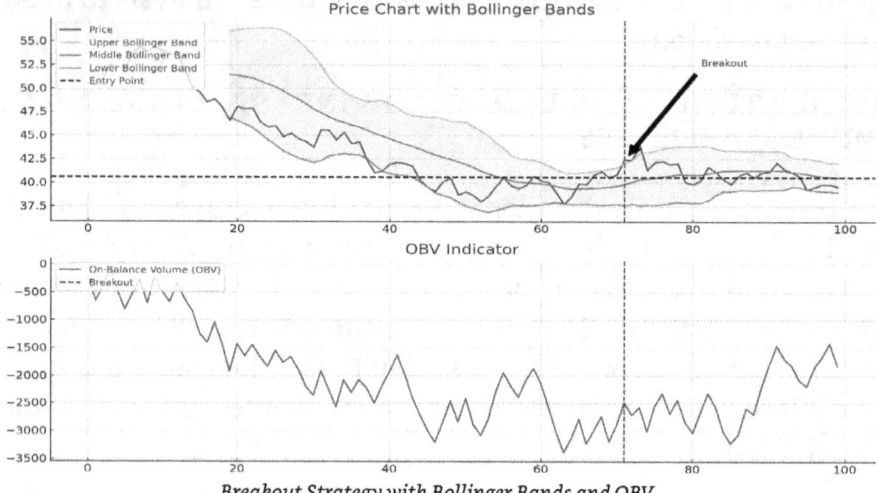

Breakout Strategy with Bollinger Bands and OBV

Outcome: The trader capitalizes on the breakout and achieves a profitable trade, using the Bollinger Bands and OBV to confirm the breakout and assess market sentiment.

CASE STUDY 3: REVERSAL STRATEGY WITH CANDLESTICK PATTERNS AND MACD

In this case study, a trader uses candlestick patterns and the MACD to identify a potential trend reversal in the natural gas market. The trader enters a long position when a bullish engulfing pattern forms at a support level, and the MACD line crosses above the signal line. The trader sets a target price based on the next resistance level.

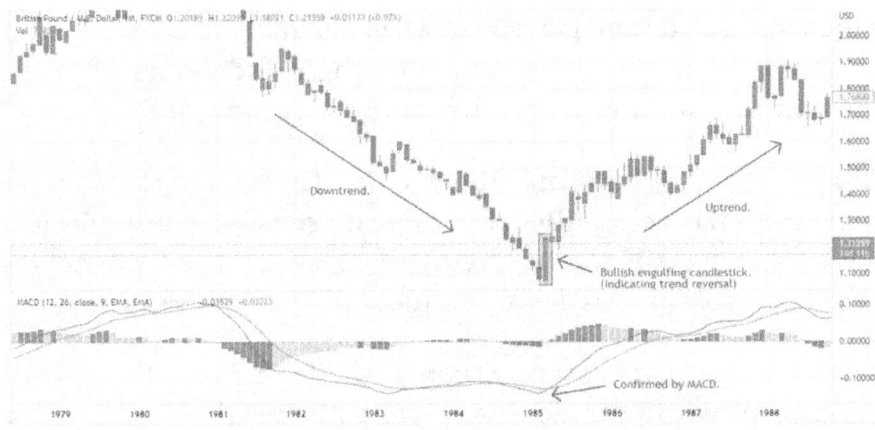

Trend Reversal with MACD: tradersunion.com

Outcome: The trader successfully identifies the trend reversal and achieves a profitable trade, using the candlestick pattern and MACD to confirm the reversal and assess trend strength.

RISKS AND LIMITATIONS OF USING TECHNICAL TOOLS

While technical tools are valuable for market decision-making, they also involve certain risks and limitations that traders should be aware of:

1. OVERRELIANCE ON TECHNICAL TOOLS

Ignoring Fundamentals: Overreliance on technical tools can lead traders to ignore fundamental factors that influence market behavior. Traders should use technical tools in conjunction with fundamental analysis to make informed decisions.

False Signals and Whipsaws: Technical tools can generate false signals and whipsaws, especially in volatile or choppy markets. Traders should use additional analysis techniques to confirm signals and reduce the risk of false trades.

2. LAGGING NATURE OF INDICATORS

Delayed Signals: Many technical indicators are based on historical data and may generate delayed signals. Traders should be aware of the lagging nature of these indicators and use them in conjunction with other analysis techniques.

Adaptation to Changing Market Conditions: Market conditions can change rapidly, affecting the reliability of technical tools. Traders should be prepared to adapt their strategies based on evolving market dynamics.

Technical tools are essential components of market decision-making, providing traders with valuable insights into market behavior and potential price movements. By understanding and applying these tools, traders can enhance their trading strategies, improve their decision-making process, and increase their chances of success in the natural gas market. However, it is essential to recognize the limitations and risks associated with technical tools and to use them in conjunction with other analysis techniques for optimal results.

PART 6: FUNDAMENTAL ANALYSIS FOR NATURAL GAS TRADING

CHAPTER 21: SUPPLY AND DEMAND FACTORS

Understanding the factors that influence the supply and demand of natural gas is crucial for traders and investors. These factors play a significant role in determining market prices and trends, and they can vary significantly due to a range of economic, geopolitical, and environmental influences. In this chapter, we will explore the key supply and demand factors affecting the natural gas market and how they impact pricing and trading decisions.

OVERVIEW OF SUPPLY FACTORS

Supply factors determine the availability of natural gas in the market. These factors include production levels, storage capacity, import and export volumes, and geopolitical considerations.

1 PRODUCTION LEVELS

Domestic Production: The level of natural gas production in a country significantly impacts its supply. Factors such as technological advancements, drilling costs, and regulatory policies influence production levels. Increased production leads to greater supply, while reduced production can cause supply shortages.

Shale Gas and Unconventional Resources: The development of shale gas and other unconventional resources has revolutionized the natural gas industry. Innovations in drilling and extraction technologies have led to significant increases in production, particularly in the United States, impacting global supply dynamics.

2. STORAGE CAPACITY

Role of Storage: Natural gas storage plays a vital role in balancing supply and demand. Storage facilities allow for the accumulation of surplus gas during periods of low demand and the release of stored gas during high-demand periods. Adequate storage capacity helps stabilize supply and prevent price spikes.

Impact of Storage Levels on Prices: High storage levels can indicate a surplus of supply, leading to lower prices. Conversely, low storage levels may signal supply constraints, resulting in higher prices. Traders monitor storage data to assess market conditions and anticipate price movements.

3. IMPORTS AND EXPORTS

Import Dependency: Countries that rely heavily on natural gas imports are influenced by global supply dynamics and geopolitical factors. Changes in import volumes can affect domestic supply levels and market prices.

Export Markets: The growth of liquefied natural gas (LNG) exports has expanded the global natural gas market. Exporting countries benefit from increased revenue and market influence, while importing countries gain access to additional supply sources.

4. GEOPOLITICAL CONSIDERATIONS

Political Stability: Political stability in major natural gas-producing regions affects supply availability. Conflicts, sanctions, and political disputes can disrupt production and exports, leading to supply shortages and price volatility.

International Relations: Diplomatic relations between producing and consuming countries influence trade agreements and supply contracts. Changes in international relations can impact import and export volumes, affecting supply dynamics.

OVERVIEW OF DEMAND FACTORS

Demand factors determine the consumption of natural gas in the market. These factors include economic growth, weather conditions, energy policies, and technological advancements.

1. ECONOMIC GROWTH

Industrial Demand: Economic growth drives industrial demand for natural gas, particularly in sectors such as manufacturing, power generation, and petrochemicals. Increased economic activity leads to higher natural gas consumption, while economic downturns result in reduced demand.

Residential and Commercial Demand: Economic conditions also influence residential and commercial demand for natural gas. Higher income levels and urbanization trends contribute to increased consumption for heating, cooking, and other domestic uses.

2. WEATHER CONDITIONS

Seasonal Variations: Weather conditions significantly impact natural gas demand, particularly for heating and cooling purposes. Cold winters increase demand for heating, while hot summers drive demand for air conditioning. Seasonal variations in demand can lead to price fluctuations and supply challenges.

Weather Forecasts and Trading: Traders closely monitor weather forecasts to anticipate changes in demand and adjust their trading strategies accordingly. Unexpected weather events, such as severe cold snaps or heatwaves, can lead to sudden spikes in demand and price volatility.

3. ENERGY POLICIES AND REGULATIONS

Government Policies: Government policies and regulations affect natural gas demand by influencing energy consumption patterns. Policies promoting renewable energy sources, energy efficiency, and emissions reductions can impact demand for natural gas.

Subsidies and Incentives: Subsidies and incentives for natural gas consumption, particularly in transportation and power generation, can stimulate demand and support market growth.

4. TECHNOLOGICAL ADVANCEMENTS

Efficiency Improvements: Technological advancements in natural gas extraction, transportation, and consumption contribute to efficiency improvements. Enhanced efficiency reduces waste and lowers costs, supporting demand growth.

Alternative Energy Sources: The development of alternative energy sources, such as solar, wind, and hydrogen, can influence natural gas demand. As these technologies become more cost-competitive and widely adopted, they may reduce the demand for natural gas.

IMPACT OF SUPPLY AND DEMAND FACTORS ON PRICES

The interplay of supply and demand factors determines natural gas prices. Understanding how these factors impact prices is essential for traders and investors.

1. PRICE VOLATILITY

Short-Term Volatility: Natural gas prices are subject to short-term volatility due to fluctuations in supply and demand. Weather events, geopolitical tensions, and changes in economic conditions can lead to rapid price movements.

Long-Term Trends: Long-term trends in supply and demand influence the overall direction of natural gas prices. For example, sustained economic growth and increased demand for cleaner energy sources can lead to upward price trends.

2. SEASONAL PRICE PATTERNS

Winter Price Spikes: Natural gas prices often experience spikes during the winter months due to increased demand for heating. Traders anticipate these seasonal patterns and adjust their strategies accordingly.

Summer Price Lulls: Conversely, natural gas prices may experience lulls during the summer months when demand for heating is low. Traders use this period to build positions and prepare for potential price increases in the winter.

3. IMPACT OF GEOPOLITICAL EVENTS

Supply Disruptions: Geopolitical events, such as conflicts, sanctions, and trade disputes, can disrupt supply and lead to price increases. Traders monitor geopolitical developments to assess their impact on supply dynamics and adjust their positions.

Market Sentiment: Geopolitical events also influence market sentiment and investor behavior. Positive developments, such as peace agreements or trade deals, can boost investor confidence and lead to price increases, while negative events can create uncertainty and downward price pressure.

STRATEGIES FOR TRADING BASED ON SUPPLY AND DE-

MAND FACTORS

Traders can develop strategies based on supply and demand factors to capitalize on market opportunities and manage risk effectively.

1. FUNDAMENTAL ANALYSIS

Supply and Demand Forecasting: Traders use fundamental analysis to forecast supply and demand dynamics and anticipate price movements. By analyzing production levels, storage data, import/export volumes, and economic indicators, traders can develop informed trading strategies.

Event-Driven Trading: Traders monitor events that impact supply and demand, such as weather forecasts, geopolitical developments, and policy changes. By assessing the potential impact of these events on the market, traders can identify trading opportunities and adjust their positions.

2. TECHNICAL ANALYSIS

Price and Volume Patterns: Traders use technical analysis to identify price and volume patterns that reflect supply and demand dynamics. For example, a breakout above a resistance level with high volume may indicate strong demand and a potential price increase.

Indicators and Oscillators: Traders use indicators and oscillators to assess market conditions and identify overbought or oversold situations. By combining technical and fundamental analysis, traders can develop comprehensive trading strategies.

3. RISK MANAGEMENT

Hedging Strategies: Traders use hedging strategies to manage risk and protect against adverse price movements. For example, a trader might use futures contracts or options to hedge against potential supply disruptions or demand fluctuations.

Stop-Loss Orders: Traders use stop-loss orders to limit potential losses and manage risk. By setting stop-loss levels based on supply and demand analysis, traders can protect their positions and minimize exposure to market volatility.

Supply and demand factors play a critical role in shaping the natural gas market and influencing prices. By understanding these factors and their impact on market dynamics, traders and investors can make informed decisions, develop effective trading strategies, and capitalize on market opportunities. However, it is essential to recognize the complexity and interdependence of supply and demand factors and to use a combination of fundamental and technical analysis for optimal results.

CHAPTER 22: ECONOMIC INDICATORS AND THEIR IMPACT

Economic indicators provide valuable insights into the overall health of the economy and can significantly influence the natural gas market. By monitoring and analyzing these indicators, traders and investors can gain a better understanding of market trends and make informed decisions. This chapter explores the key economic indicators that impact the natural gas market, their significance, and how traders can use them to their advantage.

OVERVIEW OF ECONOMIC INDICATORS

Economic indicators are statistics that provide insights into the economic performance of a country or region. These indicators are typically released by government agencies, central banks, and other authoritative sources. They help traders and investors assess the current state of the economy and anticipate future trends.

1. TYPES OF ECONOMIC INDICATORS

Leading Indicators: Leading indicators are used to predict future economic activity. They typically change before the economy as a whole begins to follow a particular trend. Examples include the Purchasing Managers' Index (PMI), consumer confidence, and stock market indices.

Coincident Indicators: Coincident indicators reflect the current state of the economy. They change simultaneously with the economic conditions they signify. Examples include GDP, industrial production, and employment levels.

Lagging Indicators: Lagging indicators are used to confirm trends in the economy that have already been established. They change after the economy has begun to follow a particular trend. Examples include the unemployment rate, corporate profits, and interest rates.

KEY ECONOMIC INDICATORS AFFECTING THE NATURAL GAS MARKET

Several economic indicators are particularly relevant to the natural gas market. Understanding these indicators and their impact can help traders and investors make more informed decisions.

1. GROSS DOMESTIC PRODUCT (GDP)

GDP measures the total value of goods and services produced within a country over a specific period. It is a primary indicator of economic health and growth. A growing GDP typically signals increased industrial activity and energy consumption, including natural gas.

Impact on Natural Gas Market: A rising GDP often leads to increased demand for natural gas, particularly in sectors such as manufacturing, transportation, and power generation. Conversely, a declining GDP may indicate reduced demand for natural gas, leading to lower prices.

2. INDUSTRIAL PRODUCTION

Industrial production measures the output of the industrial sector, including manufacturing, mining, and utilities. It is a key indicator of economic activity and energy consumption.

Impact on Natural Gas Market: Higher industrial production levels indicate increased demand for energy, including natural gas. This increased demand can lead to higher prices and greater market volatility. Traders monitor industrial production data to assess potential shifts in natural gas demand.

3. CONSUMER PRICE INDEX (CPI) AND INFLATION

The CPI measures changes in the prices of a basket of goods and services consumed by households. It is a key indicator of inflation, reflecting changes in the cost of living.

Impact on Natural Gas Market: Inflation can affect natural gas prices through changes in production costs, transportation expenses, and consumer purchasing power. Higher inflation may lead to increased natural gas prices, while lower inflation may result in price declines.

4. EMPLOYMENT DATA

Employment data, including the unemployment rate and job creation figures, provide insights into the labor market and overall economic conditions.

Impact on Natural Gas Market: Strong employment data often signals increased economic activity and energy demand, including natural gas. Conversely, weak employment data may indicate reduced energy demand and downward pressure on natural gas prices.

5. ENERGY CONSUMPTION DATA

Energy consumption data, including natural gas consumption by sector, provides insights into the overall demand for natural gas. This data is often released by government agencies and industry associations.

Impact on Natural Gas Market: Changes in energy consumption data can signal shifts in natural gas demand and supply dynamics. Traders use this data to assess market conditions and anticipate price movements.

USING ECONOMIC INDICATORS IN TRADING STRATEGIES

Traders and investors can use economic indicators to develop and refine their trading strategies. By analyzing these indicators, traders can gain insights into market trends, identify trading opportunities, and manage risk effectively.

1. FUNDAMENTAL ANALYSIS

Economic Forecasting: Traders use economic indicators to forecast economic trends and assess potential impacts on the natural gas market. By analyzing GDP, industrial production, and other indicators, traders can anticipate changes in demand and supply dynamics.

Event-Driven Trading: Traders monitor economic indicator releases and other events that impact the natural gas market. By assessing the potential impact of these events on market conditions, traders can identify trading opportunities and adjust their positions accordingly.

2. TECHNICAL ANALYSIS

Price and Volume Patterns: Traders use technical analysis to identify price and volume patterns that reflect economic trends. For example, a breakout above a resistance level with high volume may indicate strong demand and a potential price increase.

Indicators and Oscillators: Traders use indicators and oscillators to assess market conditions and identify overbought or oversold situations. By combining technical and fundamental analysis, traders can develop comprehensive trading strategies.

3. RISK MANAGEMENT

Hedging Strategies: Traders use hedging strategies to manage risk and protect against adverse price movements. For example, a trader might use futures contracts or options to hedge against potential supply disruptions or demand fluctuations.

Stop-Loss Orders: Traders use stop-loss orders to limit potential losses and manage risk. By setting stop-loss levels based on economic indicators and market analysis, traders can protect their positions and minimize exposure to market volatility.

CASE STUDIES: APPLYING ECONOMIC INDICATORS IN NATURAL GAS TRADING

To illustrate the practical application of economic indicators in natural gas trading, this section presents case studies of real-world scenarios where traders used economic analysis to make market decisions.

CASE STUDY 1: TRADING BASED ON GDP GROWTH

In this case study, a trader uses GDP data to assess the impact of economic growth on natural gas demand. The trader enters a long position in natural gas futures based on a forecast of strong GDP growth and increased industrial activity.

Outcome: The trader successfully capitalizes on the upward trend in natural gas prices, driven by increased demand and economic growth.

CASE STUDY 2: TRADING BASED ON INDUSTRIAL PRODUCTION DATA

In this case study, a trader uses industrial production data to assess the impact of manufacturing activity on natural gas demand. The trader enters a long position in natural gas options based on a forecast of increased industrial production and energy consumption.

Outcome: The trader successfully identifies a trading opportunity and achieves a profitable trade, using industrial production data to assess market conditions.

CASE STUDY 3: TRADING BASED ON INFLATION AND CPI DATA

In this case study, a trader uses CPI and inflation data to assess the impact of rising prices on natural gas demand and supply dynamics. The trader enters a short position in natural gas futures based on a forecast of rising inflation and increased production costs.

Outcome: The trader successfully navigates the market conditions and achieves a profitable trade, using CPI and inflation data to assess market sentiment.

RISKS AND LIMITATIONS OF USING ECONOMIC INDICATORS

While economic indicators provide valuable insights into market conditions, they also involve certain risks and limitations that traders should be aware of:

1. DELAYED DATA AND REVISIONS

Data Release Delays: Economic indicator data is often released with a delay, limiting its real-time applicability. Traders should be aware of the lag between data collection and release and adjust their strategies accordingly.

Revisions and Corrections: Economic indicator data is subject to revisions and corrections, which can impact market analysis and trading strategies. Traders should monitor updates and revisions to ensure accurate assessments of market conditions.

2. OVERRELIANCE ON INDICATORS

Ignoring Other Factors: Overreliance on economic indicators can lead traders to ignore other factors that influence the natural gas market. Traders should use a combination of economic, technical, and fundamental analysis to make informed decisions.

False Signals and Market Noise: Economic indicators can generate false signals and market noise, particularly in volatile or uncertain conditions. Traders should use additional analysis techniques to confirm signals and reduce the risk of false trades.

Economic indicators play a critical role in shaping the natural gas market and influencing prices. By understanding these indicators and their impact on market dynamics, traders and investors can make informed decisions, develop effective trading strategies, and capitalize on market opportunities. However, it is essential to recognize the limitations and risks associated with economic indicators and to use a combination of analysis techniques for optimal results.

CHAPTER 23: WEATHER PATTERNS AND SEASONAL INFLUENCES

Weather patterns and seasonal influences significantly impact the natural gas market, affecting both supply and demand dynamics. Understanding these factors is crucial for traders and investors as they can lead to considerable price volatility and trading opportunities. In this chapter, we will explore the role of weather and seasonal factors in the natural gas market and how traders can incorporate this information into their trading strategies.

THE IMPACT OF WEATHER ON NATURAL GAS DEMAND

Weather conditions directly influence natural gas demand, particularly for heating and cooling purposes. The natural gas market is highly sensitive to temperature changes, and even minor fluctuations can lead to significant shifts in demand.

1. WINTER WEATHER AND HEATING DEMAND

Cold Weather Impact: During the winter months, natural gas demand typically increases due to the need for heating in residential, commercial, and industrial sectors. Cold weather can lead to a spike in demand as consumers and businesses use natural gas for space heating.

Heating Degree Days (HDDs): Heating degree days (HDDs) are a measure of the demand for energy needed to heat buildings.

HDDs are calculated based on the difference between the average daily temperature and a base temperature (usually 65°F). Higher HDDs indicate greater demand for heating and, consequently, increased natural gas consumption.

Price Volatility: Cold winter weather can lead to significant price volatility in the natural gas market. Traders closely monitor weather forecasts and HDD data to anticipate changes in demand and adjust their trading strategies accordingly.

2. SUMMER WEATHER AND COOLING DEMAND

Hot Weather Impact: During the summer months, natural gas demand can increase due to the need for cooling in residential and commercial buildings. Hot weather drives demand for electricity, which is often generated using natural gas.

Cooling Degree Days (CDDs): Cooling degree days (CDDs) are a measure of the demand for energy needed to cool buildings. CDDs are calculated based on the difference between the average daily temperature and a base temperature (usually 65°F). Higher CDDs indicate greater demand for cooling and increased natural gas consumption.

Electricity Generation: Natural gas is a key fuel source for electricity generation, particularly during peak demand periods in the summer. Increased demand for electricity leads to higher natural gas consumption and can impact market prices.

SEASONAL INFLUENCES ON SUPPLY AND DEMAND

Seasonal influences play a significant role in shaping the supply and demand dynamics of the natural gas market. These influences include seasonal storage patterns, production fluctuations, and changes in consumption behavior.

1. SEASONAL STORAGE PATTERNS

Injection and Withdrawal Cycles: Natural gas storage follows a seasonal cycle, with injections typically occurring during the spring and summer months and withdrawals during the fall and winter months. This cycle helps balance supply and demand and stabilize prices.

Impact on Prices: Storage levels and injection/withdrawal rates can impact natural gas prices. High storage levels can indicate a surplus of supply, leading to lower prices, while low storage levels may signal supply constraints and result in higher prices.

2. PRODUCTION FLUCTUATIONS

Seasonal Production Variations: Natural gas production can vary seasonally due to factors such as weather-related disruptions, maintenance activities, and changes in demand. For example, hurricanes and other severe weather events can disrupt production in offshore and coastal regions, leading to supply constraints.

Impact on Prices: Seasonal production fluctuations can impact natural gas prices by affecting supply levels. Traders monitor production data and weather forecasts to assess potential disruptions and anticipate price movements.

3. CHANGES IN CONSUMPTION BEHAVIOR

Residential and Commercial Demand: Seasonal changes in consumption behavior, such as increased heating demand in the winter and cooling demand in the summer, impact natural gas demand. These changes can lead to fluctuations in prices and market volatility.

Industrial Demand: Industrial demand for natural gas can also vary seasonally due to factors such as production schedules, maintenance activities, and changes in energy consumption patterns. Traders assess these factors to anticipate changes in demand and adjust their trading strategies.

WEATHER FORECASTING AND ITS ROLE IN TRADING

Weather forecasting plays a critical role in natural gas trading, as it provides valuable insights into potential changes in demand and supply dynamics. Traders use weather forecasts to assess market conditions, identify trading opportunities, and manage risk.

1. TYPES OF WEATHER FORECASTS

Short-Term Forecasts: Short-term weather forecasts provide predictions for the next few days to a week. These forecasts are used to assess immediate changes in demand and supply dynamics and to make short-term trading decisions.

Medium-Term Forecasts: Medium-term weather forecasts provide predictions for the next few weeks to a month. These forecasts help traders assess potential changes in demand and supply dynamics over a longer period and adjust their trading strategies accordingly.

Long-Term Forecasts: Long-term weather forecasts provide predictions for the next few months to a year. These forecasts are used to assess potential changes in demand and supply dynamics over a longer period and to develop longer-term trading strategies.

2. WEATHER MODELS AND DATA SOURCES

Numerical Weather Prediction Models: Numerical weather prediction models use mathematical equations to simulate the behavior of the atmosphere and predict future weather conditions. These models are used by meteorologists and traders to assess potential changes in demand and supply dynamics.

Weather Data Providers: Weather data providers, such as the National Weather Service (NWS), the European Centre for Medium-Range Weather Forecasts (ECMWF), and private weather forecasting companies, provide weather data and forecasts to traders and investors. Traders use this data to assess market conditions and make informed decisions.

3. INCORPORATING WEATHER FORECASTS INTO TRADING STRATEGIES

Anticipating Demand Changes: Traders use weather forecasts to anticipate changes in demand for natural gas and adjust their trading strategies accordingly. For example, a forecast of colder-than-average temperatures may lead traders to expect increased heating demand and higher natural gas prices.

Assessing Supply Disruptions: Traders use weather forecasts to assess potential supply disruptions, such as hurricanes or other severe weather events, and adjust their trading strategies accordingly. For example, a forecast of a major hurricane in the Gulf of Mexico may lead traders to expect production disruptions and higher natural gas prices.

Managing Risk: Traders use weather forecasts to manage risk and protect against adverse price movements. For example, a trader might use futures contracts or options to hedge against potential supply disruptions or demand fluctuations.

CASE STUDIES: WEATHER AND SEASONAL INFLUENCES ON NATURAL GAS TRADING

To illustrate the practical application of weather and seasonal influences in natural gas trading, this section presents case studies of real-world scenarios where traders used weather forecasts and seasonal data to make market decisions.

CASE STUDY 1: TRADING BASED ON WINTER WEATHER FORECASTS

In this case study, a trader uses winter weather forecasts to assess the impact of colder-than-average temperatures on natural gas demand. The trader enters a long position in natural gas futures based on a forecast of increased heating demand and higher prices.

Outcome: The trader successfully capitalizes on the upward trend in natural gas prices, driven by increased demand and colder-than-average temperatures.

CASE STUDY 2: TRADING BASED ON SUMMER COOLING DEMAND

In this case study, a trader uses summer weather forecasts to assess the impact of hotter-than-average temperatures on natural gas demand for cooling purposes. The trader enters a long position in natural gas options based on a forecast of increased electricity demand and higher prices.

Outcome: The trader successfully identifies a trading opportunity and achieves a profitable trade, using summer weather forecasts to assess market conditions.

CASE STUDY 3: TRADING BASED ON SEASONAL STORAGE PATTERNS

In this case study, a trader uses data on seasonal storage patterns to assess the impact of low storage levels on natural gas prices. The trader enters a long position in natural gas futures based on a forecast of supply constraints and higher prices.

Outcome: The trader successfully navigates the market conditions and achieves a profitable trade, using seasonal storage data to assess market sentiment.

RISKS AND LIMITATIONS OF USING WEATHER AND SEASONAL DATA

While weather and seasonal data provide valuable insights into the natural gas market, they also involve certain risks and limitations that traders should be aware of:

1. UNCERTAINTY AND FORECAST ERRORS

Uncertainty in Weather Forecasts: Weather forecasts are inherently uncertain, and forecast errors can lead to inaccurate assessments of market conditions. Traders should be aware of the limitations of weather forecasts and adjust their strategies accordingly.

Impact of Forecast Errors on Prices: Forecast errors can lead to significant price volatility and market uncertainty. Traders should use additional analysis techniques to confirm weather forecasts and reduce the risk of false trades.

2. OVERRELIANCE ON SEASONAL DATA

Ignoring Other Factors: Overreliance on seasonal data can lead traders to ignore other factors that influence the natural gas market. Traders should use a combination of weather, seasonal, technical, and fundamental analysis to make informed decisions.

Market Noise and False Signals: Seasonal data can generate false signals and market noise, particularly in volatile or uncertain conditions. Traders should use additional analysis techniques to confirm signals and reduce the risk of false trades.

Weather patterns and seasonal influences play a critical role in shaping the natural gas market and influencing prices.

By understanding these factors and their impact on market dynamics, traders and investors can make informed decisions, develop effective trading strategies, and capitalize on market opportunities.

However, it is essential to recognize the limitations and risks associated with weather and seasonal data and to use a combination of analysis techniques for optimal results.

The natural gas market's sensitivity to weather conditions and seasonal patterns makes it a complex and dynamic environment. Traders and investors who can effectively navigate these challenges by using comprehensive data analysis and risk management strategies will be better positioned to achieve success in the natural gas market.

CHAPTER 24: GEOPOLITICAL EVENTS AND THEIR EFFECTS ON PRICES

Natural gas prices are influenced by a myriad of factors, and among the most significant are geopolitical events. These events, often unpredictable and sudden, can lead to rapid fluctuations in natural gas prices, impacting both short-term and long-term market dynamics. In this chapter, we will explore the various geopolitical factors that affect natural gas markets and examine how traders and investors can anticipate and respond to these events.

UNDERSTANDING GEOPOLITICAL RISKS

Geopolitical risks encompass a broad range of events, including conflicts, policy changes, and international relations. These risks can affect the natural gas market by disrupting supply chains, altering demand patterns, or changing market perceptions.

TYPES OF GEOPOLITICAL EVENTS

Conflicts and Wars: Military conflicts and wars in major natural gas-producing regions can disrupt production and transportation, leading to supply shortages and increased prices. For example, conflicts in the Middle East or Eastern Europe can significantly impact global natural gas markets.

Sanctions and Trade Disputes: Economic sanctions and trade disputes between countries can affect natural gas exports and imports. Sanctions on major gas-producing countries or companies can limit supply availability, causing price spikes.

Political Instability: Political instability in gas-producing or transit countries can create uncertainty in the market. Changes in government, policy shifts, or social unrest can impact production levels and export capabilities.

Regulatory Changes: Changes in energy policies or regulations in major consuming or producing countries can influence natural gas demand and supply dynamics. Policies promoting renewable energy or imposing restrictions on fossil fuels can affect natural gas consumption and prices.

OPEC+ Decisions: Although OPEC primarily focuses on oil, its decisions can indirectly impact natural gas markets. For instance, agreements on production cuts or increases can affect energy prices and market sentiment.

IMPACT OF GEOPOLITICAL RISKS ON PRICES

Geopolitical events can lead to significant price volatility in the natural gas market. Traders and investors need to understand how these events influence market dynamics to make informed decisions. Some key impacts include:

Supply Disruptions: Geopolitical events that disrupt supply chains can lead to immediate shortages and price spikes. For example, conflicts in the Middle East or disruptions in pipelines can reduce supply and increase prices.

Demand Shifts: Geopolitical tensions can affect global energy demand patterns. For instance, sanctions on a major gas producer can lead to increased demand from alternative sources, driving up prices.

Market Sentiment: Geopolitical risks can influence market sentiment, leading to speculative trading and increased volatility. Traders often respond to perceived risks by adjusting their positions, which can amplify price movements.

CASE STUDIES: GEOPOLITICAL EVENTS AND THEIR EFFECTS

This section examines real-world case studies to illustrate how geopolitical events have impacted natural gas prices and market dynamics.

CASE STUDY 1: THE RUSSIA-UKRAINE CONFLICT

Background: The ongoing conflict between Russia and Ukraine has had a significant impact on natural gas markets, given Russia's role as a major gas supplier to Europe. Disruptions in gas flows through Ukraine have raised concerns about supply security in Europe.

Impact on Prices: The conflict has led to increased price volatility, with concerns about supply disruptions causing price spikes. European countries have sought alternative sources of gas, including LNG imports, to reduce reliance on Russian gas.

Market Response: Traders have closely monitored developments in the conflict, adjusting their positions based on changes in supply and demand dynamics. The conflict has also prompted increased investment in LNG infrastructure and renewable energy sources in Europe.

CASE STUDY 2: U.S. SANCTIONS ON IRAN

Background: The U.S. has imposed sanctions on Iran's energy sector, targeting its oil and gas exports. These sanctions have affected Iran's ability to export natural gas, impacting global supply levels.

Impact on Prices: The sanctions have reduced the availability of Iranian gas in the global market, leading to concerns about supply shortages and increased prices. The sanctions have also affected global trade flows, with countries seeking alternative sources of gas.

Market Response: Traders have reacted to the sanctions by adjusting their positions and seeking opportunities in alternative markets. The sanctions have also prompted increased investment in LNG projects and pipeline infrastructure to diversify supply sources.

CASE STUDY 3: THE COVID-19 PANDEMIC

Background: The COVID-19 pandemic has had a profound impact on global energy markets, including natural gas. Lockdowns and restrictions on travel and industrial activity have led to significant shifts in demand and supply dynamics.

Impact on Prices: The pandemic initially led to a sharp decline in natural gas demand, causing prices to plummet. However, as economies reopened and demand recovered, prices rebounded, driven by supply constraints and increased consumption.

Market Response: Traders have had to navigate unprecedented market conditions, using a combination of fundamental and technical analysis to assess market trends. The pandemic has also highlighted the importance of supply chain resilience and diversification in the natural gas market.

STRATEGIES FOR MANAGING GEOPOLITICAL RISKS

Managing geopolitical risks is crucial for traders and investors in the natural gas market. Here are some strategies to consider:

1. DIVERSIFICATION

Diversify Supply Sources: Diversifying supply sources can help mitigate the impact of supply disruptions caused by geopolitical events. Traders and investors should consider investing in a mix of domestic and international supply sources, including LNG and pipeline gas.

Diversify Trading Strategies: Diversifying trading strategies can help reduce exposure to geopolitical risks. Traders should consider using a combination of futures, options, and other derivatives to manage risk and capitalize on market opportunities.

2. HEDGING

Use of Derivatives: Hedging with futures, options, and other derivatives can help protect against price volatility caused by geopolitical events. Traders can use these instruments to lock in prices or limit potential losses.

Currency Hedging: Geopolitical events can also impact currency markets, affecting the value of natural gas contracts denominated in different currencies. Traders should consider using currency hedging strategies to manage exchange rate risk.

3. MONITORING AND ANALYSIS

Stay Informed: Staying informed about geopolitical developments is crucial for managing risk in the natural gas market. Traders should monitor news and analysis from reliable sources to stay ahead of market trends.

Use of Analytics Tools: Using analytics tools and data platforms can help traders assess the impact of geopolitical events on market dynamics. Traders can use these tools to analyze historical data, model scenarios, and identify potential risks and opportunities.

Geopolitical events are a significant factor in the natural gas market, influencing prices and market dynamics. By understanding the various geopolitical risks and their potential impact, traders and investors can make informed decisions and develop effective strategies to manage risk and capitalize on market opportunities.

However, it is essential to recognize the uncertainties and complexities associated with geopolitical events and to use a combination of analysis techniques and risk management strategies for optimal results.

PART 7: DEVELOPING A TRADING STRATEGY

CHAPTER 25: RISK MANAGEMENT AND POSITION SIZING

In the volatile world of natural gas trading, managing risk effectively is essential for long-term success. Whether you are a beginner or a seasoned trader, understanding and implementing risk management strategies can help you protect your capital, minimize losses, and maximize profits. This chapter will explore the key principles of risk management and position sizing, providing practical guidance for traders in the natural gas market.

THE IMPORTANCE OF RISK MANAGEMENT

Risk management is a critical component of any trading strategy. It involves identifying, assessing, and mitigating potential risks to minimize the impact of adverse market movements on your portfolio. Effective risk management can help you avoid significant losses and preserve your trading capital, allowing you to stay in the game and take advantage of future opportunities.

TYPES OF RISKS IN NATURAL GAS TRADING

Market Risk: Market risk refers to the potential for losses due to unfavorable price movements in the natural gas market. This risk is inherent in all trading activities and can be caused by various factors, including supply and demand dynamics, geopolitical events, and economic indicators.

Credit Risk: Credit risk is the risk of loss resulting from the failure of a counterparty to fulfill its contractual obligations. In the natural gas market, credit risk can arise from counterparties failing to deliver gas or pay for it, particularly in volatile or uncertain market conditions.

Liquidity Risk: Liquidity risk is the risk of not being able to buy or sell natural gas contracts at the desired price due to a lack of market participants or trading volume. This risk can be particularly acute in less liquid markets or during periods of market stress.

Operational Risk: Operational risk is the risk of loss due to failures in internal processes, systems, or controls. This risk can arise from human error, technical failures, or inadequate risk management practices.

Regulatory Risk: Regulatory risk is the risk of loss due to changes in laws, regulations, or policies that affect the natural gas market. This risk can impact trading activities, pricing, and market dynamics.

BENEFITS OF EFFECTIVE RISK MANAGEMENT

Effective risk management offers several benefits for natural gas traders, including:

Capital Preservation: By managing risk effectively, traders can protect their capital and avoid significant losses that could jeopardize their trading activities.

Reduced Volatility: Risk management strategies can help traders reduce the volatility of their portfolios, leading to more stable returns and lower stress levels.

Improved Decision-Making: By identifying and assessing potential risks, traders can make more informed decisions and develop strategies that align with their risk tolerance and investment objectives.

Increased Confidence: Implementing risk management practices can help traders build confidence in their trading strategies and approach, leading to better performance and outcomes.

KEY RISK MANAGEMENT STRATEGIES

There are several risk management strategies that traders can use to manage their exposure to market risks. These strategies can be tailored to individual preferences and risk tolerance levels, providing a flexible approach to risk management.

1. SETTING STOP-LOSS ORDERS

A stop-loss order is an order to sell a security or exit a position if the price reaches a specified level. This order helps traders limit their losses by automatically closing a position when the market moves against them.

Implementation: Traders can set stop-loss orders at a predetermined price level based on their risk tolerance and market analysis. For example, a trader may set a stop-loss order at 5% below their entry price to limit potential losses.

Benefits: Stop-loss orders provide a simple and effective way to manage risk by preventing significant losses and preserving capital. They also help traders avoid emotional decision-making by automating the exit process.

2. USING TAKE-PROFIT ORDERS

A take-profit order is an order to sell a security or close a position when the price reaches a specified level of profit. This order helps traders lock in profits and exit positions at favorable price levels.

Implementation: Traders can set take-profit orders based on their profit targets and market analysis. For example, a trader may set a take-profit order at 10% above their entry price to secure profits.

Benefits: Take-profit orders allow traders to capitalize on favorable market movements and secure profits without having to constantly monitor the market. They also help traders avoid the temptation to hold onto winning positions for too long, which can lead to losses if the market reverses.

3. DIVERSIFICATION

Diversification is the practice of spreading investments across different assets, markets, or strategies to reduce risk. By diversifying their portfolios, traders can mitigate the impact of adverse market movements on individual positions.

Implementation: Traders can diversify their portfolios by investing in a mix of natural gas contracts, including spot contracts, futures contracts, and options. They can also consider diversifying across different markets, such as oil, electricity, or other commodities.

Benefits: Diversification helps traders reduce the volatility of their portfolios and protect against significant losses from individual positions. It also provides exposure to different market opportunities and can enhance overall returns.

4. HEDGING

Hedging is a risk management strategy that involves taking offsetting positions in different assets or markets to reduce exposure to adverse price movements. Hedging can help traders manage risk and protect their portfolios from market volatility.

Implementation: Traders can use various hedging strategies, such as buying put options to protect against price declines or selling call options to generate income. They can also consider using futures contracts to lock in prices or offset positions in different markets.

Benefits: Hedging provides a flexible and effective way to manage risk and protect against adverse market movements. It also allows traders to take advantage of different market conditions and opportunities.

POSITION SIZING AND ITS ROLE IN RISK MANAGEMENT

Position sizing is a crucial aspect of risk management that involves determining the appropriate size of a trading position based on the trader's risk tolerance and market conditions. Proper position sizing can help traders manage risk effectively and optimize their returns.

1. FACTORS TO CONSIDER IN POSITION SIZING

Risk Tolerance: Risk tolerance refers to the trader's willingness to accept losses and exposure to market risks. Traders should consider their risk tolerance when determining the size of their positions, as larger positions can lead to higher potential losses.

Market Volatility: Market volatility refers to the degree of price fluctuations in the natural gas market. Traders should consider market volatility when sizing their positions, as higher volatility can lead to larger price swings and increased risk.

Account Size: Account size refers to the total value of the trader's portfolio or trading account. Traders should consider their account size when determining the size of their positions, as larger positions can consume more capital and increase exposure to market risks.

Stop-Loss Levels: Stop-loss levels refer to the price levels at which traders set their stop-loss orders. Traders should consider their stop-loss levels when sizing their positions, as larger positions can lead to higher potential losses if the market moves against them.

2. POSITION SIZING STRATEGIES

There are several position sizing strategies that traders can use to manage risk and optimize their returns. These strategies can be tailored to individual preferences and risk tolerance levels, providing a flexible approach to position sizing.

Fixed Percentage Risk: This strategy involves determining the size of a position based on a fixed percentage of the trader's account size. For example, a trader may decide to risk 1% of their account on each trade, which helps to limit potential losses and preserve capital.

Volatility-Based Position Sizing: This strategy involves determining the size of a position based on market volatility. Traders can use indicators such as the Average True Range (ATR) to assess market volatility and adjust their position sizes accordingly. For example, a trader may reduce their position size in highly volatile markets to manage risk effectively.

Capital Allocation: This strategy involves allocating a specific amount of capital to different positions based on their risk-reward profiles. Traders can use this approach to optimize their returns and manage risk by investing in a mix of high-risk, high-reward positions and low-risk, low-reward positions.

Risk management and position sizing are critical components of a successful trading strategy in the natural gas market. By understanding and implementing these strategies, traders can protect their capital, minimize losses, and optimize their returns. Whether you are a beginner or a seasoned trader, risk management should be a top priority in your trading activities.

CHAPTER 26: COMBINING TECHNICAL AND FUNDAMENTAL ANALYSIS

In the world of natural gas trading, both technical and fundamental analysis play crucial roles in helping traders make informed decisions. While each approach has its unique advantages and limitations, combining these methods can provide a comprehensive view of the market and enhance trading strategies. In this chapter, we will explore how to integrate technical and fundamental analysis to improve your trading performance in the natural gas market.

UNDERSTANDING THE TWO APPROACHES

Before diving into how to combine technical and fundamental analysis, it's essential to understand the core principles of each approach and their respective strengths and weaknesses.

1. TECHNICAL ANALYSIS

Technical analysis is the study of past market data, primarily price and volume, to predict future price movements. It relies on charts and various technical indicators to identify patterns, trends, and signals that can inform trading decisions. Key aspects of technical analysis include:

Chart Patterns: Technical analysts use chart patterns, such as head and shoulders, triangles, and double tops, to identify potential price movements and trend reversals.

Indicators: Common technical indicators include moving averages, relative strength index (RSI), moving average convergence divergence (MACD), and Bollinger Bands. These tools help traders gauge market momentum, volatility, and overbought or oversold conditions.

Support and Resistance Levels: Technical analysts identify support and resistance levels, which are price points where the market tends to pause or reverse direction. These levels help traders determine entry and exit points.

2. FUNDAMENTAL ANALYSIS

Fundamental analysis evaluates the intrinsic value of an asset based on economic, financial, and industry-related factors. In the context of natural gas trading, fundamental analysis involves assessing supply and demand dynamics, economic indicators, geopolitical events, and company performance. Key aspects of fundamental analysis include:

Supply and Demand: Traders analyze factors affecting natural gas supply and demand, such as production levels, weather patterns, and storage data, to predict price movements.

Economic Indicators: Economic indicators, such as GDP growth, inflation, and interest rates, can influence natural gas prices by affecting demand and production costs.

Geopolitical Events: Geopolitical events, such as conflicts, trade agreements, and regulatory changes, can significantly impact natural gas prices and market dynamics.

BENEFITS OF COMBINING TECHNICAL AND FUNDAMENTAL ANALYSIS

Combining technical and fundamental analysis offers several benefits for natural gas traders, including:

Comprehensive Market View: Integrating both approaches

provides a more comprehensive view of the market, helping traders identify opportunities and risks that may not be apparent when using only one method.

Enhanced Decision-Making: By combining technical and fundamental analysis, traders can make more informed decisions based on a broader range of data and insights.

Improved Risk Management: A combined approach can help traders manage risk more effectively by providing a better understanding of market conditions and potential price movements.

Increased Confidence: Using a combination of technical and fundamental analysis can increase traders' confidence in their strategies and decisions, leading to better performance and outcomes.

STRATEGIES FOR COMBINING TECHNICAL AND FUNDAMENTAL ANALYSIS

There are several strategies that traders can use to combine technical and fundamental analysis effectively. These strategies can be tailored to individual preferences and trading styles, providing a flexible approach to market analysis.

1. CONFIRMATION AND VALIDATION

One of the simplest ways to combine technical and fundamental analysis is to use one method to confirm or validate the other. For example, traders can use fundamental analysis to identify potential opportunities or risks and then use technical analysis to confirm the timing of their trades.

Identify Fundamental Trends: Traders can start by identifying fundamental trends, such as changes in supply and demand dynamics or economic indicators. These trends can provide insights into potential price movements and market conditions.

Use Technical Analysis for Timing: Once a fundamental trend has been identified, traders can use technical analysis to determine the optimal entry and exit points for their trades. This approach helps traders capitalize on fundamental trends while minimizing risk.

2. INTEGRATING TECHNICAL AND FUNDAMENTAL SIGNALS

Another strategy for combining technical and fundamental analysis is to integrate signals from both approaches into a single trading strategy. Traders can develop rules or criteria that incorporate technical indicators and fundamental data, allowing them to make more informed decisions based on a combination of factors.

Develop a Trading Plan: Traders can develop a trading plan that outlines specific criteria for entering and exiting trades based on a combination of technical and fundamental signals. For example, a trader may decide to enter a long position if a technical indicator shows an upward trend and a fundamental analysis indicates strong demand.

Monitor and Adjust: Traders should regularly monitor their trading plan and adjust it as needed based on changes in market conditions or new data. This approach helps traders stay flexible and responsive to evolving market dynamics.

3. SCENARIO ANALYSIS

Scenario analysis involves evaluating different potential market scenarios based on a combination of technical and fundamental factors. Traders can use scenario analysis to assess the potential impact of various events or conditions on natural gas prices and market dynamics.

Identify Key Variables: Traders can start by identifying key variables that could impact the market, such as changes in supply and demand, economic indicators, or geopolitical events. These variables can provide a framework for evaluating different scenarios.

Evaluate Potential Outcomes: Once key variables have been identified, traders can evaluate the potential outcomes of different scenarios based on a combination of technical and fundamental analysis. For example, a trader may assess the impact of a supply disruption on prices by analyzing technical indicators and fundamental data.

Develop Contingency Plans: Traders can develop contingency plans for different scenarios, outlining specific actions or strategies they would take in each case. This approach helps traders prepare for potential market changes and manage risk effectively.

CASE STUDIES: SUCCESSFUL INTEGRATION OF TECHNICAL AND FUNDAMENTAL ANALYSIS

This section examines real-world case studies to illustrate how traders have successfully integrated technical and fundamental analysis in the natural gas market.

CASE STUDY 1: THE IMPACT OF WEATHER PATTERNS

Background: In the winter of 2021, severe weather conditions in the United States led to increased demand for natural gas for heating. This demand surge was accompanied by supply constraints due to pipeline disruptions and production shutdowns.

Fundamental Analysis: Traders who conducted fundamental analysis identified the potential impact of weather patterns on natural gas demand and supply. They assessed factors such as temperature forecasts, storage levels, and production disruptions to gauge the market's response.

Technical Analysis: Technical analysts used indicators such as moving averages, RSI, and Bollinger Bands to identify entry and exit points based on price movements and market trends. They also monitored support and resistance levels to determine potential price targets.

Outcome: By combining technical and fundamental analysis, traders were able to capitalize on the market's response to the weather conditions, entering and exiting positions at optimal times and maximizing their returns.

CASE STUDY 2: THE ROLE OF GEOPOLITICAL EVENTS

Background: In early 2022, escalating tensions between Russia and Ukraine led to concerns about potential supply disruptions in the European natural gas market. These concerns were compounded by regulatory changes and sanctions imposed by the United States and the European Union.

Fundamental Analysis: Traders who conducted fundamental analysis assessed the potential impact of geopolitical events on natural gas supply and demand. They evaluated factors such as pipeline routes, export capacities, and regulatory developments to gauge the market's response.

Technical Analysis: Technical analysts used indicators such as MACD, stochastic oscillators, and Fibonacci retracements to identify entry and exit points based on price movements and market trends. They also monitored volume and open interest to assess market sentiment and liquidity.

Outcome: By combining technical and fundamental analysis, traders were able to navigate the market's response to the geopolitical events, entering and exiting positions at optimal times and managing their risk effectively.

Combining technical and fundamental analysis is a powerful

approach to natural gas trading, providing traders with a comprehensive view of the market and enhancing their decision-making process. By integrating these methods, traders can identify opportunities and risks more effectively, optimize their trading strategies, and improve their overall performance.

CHAPTER 27: BACKTESTING YOUR STRATEGY

Backtesting is an essential step in the development and refinement of any trading strategy. By simulating how your trading strategy would have performed using historical data, you can gain valuable insights into its potential effectiveness, identify any weaknesses or limitations, and refine it to improve future performance. In this chapter, we will explore the process of backtesting, the tools and techniques used, and the benefits and limitations of this approach.

THE IMPORTANCE OF BACKTESTING

Validating Your Strategy: Backtesting allows you to test your trading strategy using historical data to see how it would have performed in the past. This process helps validate your strategy's potential profitability and highlights any weaknesses.

Tip: Consistently backtest your strategies before implementing them in live trading to ensure they are robust and reliable.

Reducing Risk: By identifying potential flaws in your strategy through backtesting, you can reduce the risk of losses when trading with real money. This preemptive approach helps you avoid costly mistakes and improves your overall risk management.

Tip: Pay attention to how your strategy performs during different market conditions, such as bull, bear, and sideways markets, to ensure it's adaptable.

HOW TO BACKTEST YOUR STRATEGY

Choosing the Right Software: To backtest effectively, you'll need to use trading software that allows you to apply your strategy to historical data. Many trading platforms offer built-in backtesting tools, while others require third-party software.

Tip: Select a platform that provides comprehensive historical data and detailed performance metrics. Ensure the software is user-friendly and meets your specific needs.

Setting Up Your Parameters: Before running a backtest, you need to define the parameters of your strategy, such as entry and exit points, stop-loss levels, and position sizing. Clearly outlining these rules will help ensure that your backtest is accurate and reflective of your strategy's real-world application.

Tip: Be consistent with your parameters during the backtesting process. Avoid making changes midway, as this can skew results and reduce the accuracy of your findings.

Running the Backtest: Once your parameters are set, you can run the backtest by applying your strategy to the selected historical data. The software will simulate trades based on your rules and generate results that show how the strategy would have performed.

Tip: Run multiple backtests across different time periods and market conditions to ensure your strategy is versatile and can perform consistently.

INTERPRETING BACKTEST RESULTS

Key Metrics to Analyze: When reviewing backtest results, focus on key performance metrics such as profitability, drawdown, win/loss ratio, and risk-adjusted returns. These metrics will provide insights into the strategy's strengths and weaknesses.

Tip: Pay particular attention to drawdown, as this indicates the maximum potential loss from peak to trough in your strategy's performance. A high drawdown may suggest that the strategy carries too much risk.

Identifying Patterns and Anomalies: Analyzing the results of your backtest can reveal patterns or anomalies that might not be apparent in live trading. For example, your strategy may perform well in trending markets but struggle during periods of low volatility.

Tip: Use these insights to refine your strategy. If you identify a consistent issue, consider adjusting your parameters or incorporating additional indicators to improve performance.

Stress Testing Your Strategy: In addition to standard backtesting, stress testing involves applying your strategy to extreme market conditions to see how it holds up under pressure. This can help you understand potential risks and prepare for worst-case scenarios.

Tip: Simulate conditions such as market crashes or periods of high volatility to assess how your strategy would perform. Make necessary adjustments to ensure your strategy is resilient.

REFINING YOUR STRATEGY BASED ON BACKTEST RESULTS

Making Data-Driven Adjustments: Use the data from your backtests to make informed adjustments to your strategy. This might involve tweaking your entry and exit rules, adjusting stop-loss levels, or re-evaluating your risk management approach.

Tip: Focus on gradual, incremental changes rather than overhauling your strategy entirely. Small adjustments can often lead to significant improvements in performance.

Avoiding Overfitting: Overfitting occurs when a strategy is too closely tailored to historical data, resulting in poor performance in live trading. To avoid this, ensure your strategy is flexible and not overly optimized for specific market conditions.

Tip: Test your strategy on out-of-sample data—historical data that was not used during the initial backtest—to ensure it performs well in different market environments.

Continuous Monitoring and Improvement: Backtesting is not a one-time process. Continually monitor your strategy's performance and make adjustments as needed. As market conditions change, your strategy should evolve to stay effective.

Tip: Regularly revisit your backtest results and refine your strategy based on new data and market developments. Continuous improvement is key to long-term success.

TRANSITIONING FROM BACKTESTING TO LIVE TRADING

Testing in a Demo Environment: After successful backtesting, consider testing your strategy in a demo environment. This allows you to apply your strategy in live market conditions without risking real money.

Tip: Use this phase to gain confidence in your strategy and to further refine your approach based on real-time feedback.

Starting with Small Positions: When you're ready to move from demo trading to live trading, start with small positions. This cautious approach allows you to test your strategy in real market conditions while minimizing potential losses.

Tip: Gradually increase your position size as you gain more confidence in your strategy's performance in live trading.

Backtesting is an essential tool for any trader looking to refine their strategies and achieve long-term success in the natural gas market. By rigorously testing your approach using historical data, analyzing the results, and making data-driven adjustments, you can develop a robust and effective trading strategy. Remember, backtesting is an ongoing process that should be revisited regularly to ensure your strategy remains relevant and profitable as market conditions evolve.

CHAPTER 28: BUILDING A TRADING PLAN

A trading plan is a comprehensive and personalized document that outlines your approach to trading in the natural gas market. It serves as a blueprint for your trading activities, detailing your strategies, goals, risk management rules, and the processes you will follow. A well-structured trading plan provides clarity, consistency, and discipline, helping you navigate the complexities of the market with confidence and purpose.

In this chapter, we'll explore the essential components of a trading plan, how to develop one that aligns with your trading style and goals, and the importance of adhering to your plan for long-term success.

WHAT IS A TRADING PLAN?

A trading plan is a written document that guides your trading activities. It includes your trading strategy, risk management guidelines, financial goals, and the specific rules you will follow. The purpose of a trading plan is to provide a structured approach to trading, ensuring that your decisions are based on careful analysis and a clear set of criteria rather than on emotions or impulses. By following a trading plan, you can improve your trading discipline, manage risk more effectively, and increase your chances of achieving your financial objectives.

KEY ELEMENTS OF A TRADING PLAN

A trading plan is a structured guide that outlines how you will engage in trading activities. It is essential to ensure consistency, discipline, and a strategic approach to trading. Below are the key elements that form the foundation of a comprehensive trading plan:

1. TRADING STRATEGY

Your trading strategy is your overall approach to analyzing the market and identifying potential trading opportunities. It encompasses the methods, tools, and criteria you use to decide when to enter and exit trades.

Key Components:

Market Analysis: Define whether you will use technical analysis, fundamental analysis, or a combination of both. Identify the tools and indicators that will aid your analysis.

Trade Selection: Specify the criteria that must be met before you initiate a trade. This might include certain patterns, indicators, or price levels.

Entry and Exit Points: Clearly define the conditions under which you will enter and exit trades. This helps prevent emotional decisions and ensures consistency in your trading approach.

Timeframes: Determine the timeframes you will use for trading, such as intraday, daily, or weekly charts.

Example: A trader might use a combination of moving averages and support and resistance levels to identify trends and determine entry and exit points.

2. RISK MANAGEMENT

Risk management involves setting guidelines to manage and minimize potential losses in your trading activities. It includes strategies for determining position sizes, setting stop-loss levels, and limiting your overall exposure to the market.

Key Components:

Position Sizing: Establish rules for how much capital you will allocate to each trade. This should be based on your overall risk tolerance and the size of your trading account.

Stop-Loss Orders: Determine the level at which you will exit a losing trade to prevent further losses. This is a critical tool for protecting your capital.

Maximum Exposure: Set limits on how much of your total trading capital you are willing to risk at any given time. This helps prevent significant losses that could jeopardize your trading account.

Risk-Reward Ratio: Define the minimum acceptable risk-reward ratio for your trades. This ensures that the potential reward justifies the risk taken.

Example: A trader might decide to risk no more than 1% of their trading account on any single trade and set a stop-loss order to automatically close a position if it moves against them by a specified amount.

3. FINANCIAL GOALS

Financial goals are specific, measurable objectives that you aim to achieve through your trading activities. These goals provide direction and help you stay focused on your long-term trading plan.

Key Components:

Short-Term Goals: These are targets you aim to achieve within a shorter timeframe, such as weekly or monthly. They help keep you motivated and provide milestones to track your progress.

Long-Term Goals: These are broader objectives that you aim to achieve over an extended period, such as yearly goals or building a diversified portfolio.

Realistic Expectations: Ensure that your goals are achievable based on your trading strategy, risk tolerance, and market conditions. Unrealistic goals can lead to frustration and poor trading decisions.

Example: A trader might set a short-term goal of achieving a 5% monthly return on their trading account and a long-term goal of doubling their account size within two years.

4. TRADING ROUTINE

A trading routine is a schedule and process for conducting your trading activities. It includes regular tasks such as market analysis, strategy reviews, and performance evaluations.

Key Components:

Daily or Weekly Schedule: Outline the specific times when you will conduct market analysis, place trades, and review your performance. Consistency is crucial for developing good trading habits.

Pre-Market Analysis: Identify the key factors you will review before the market opens, such as news events, technical indicators, and market trends.

Post-Market Review: Conduct a regular review of your trades and performance, assessing what went well and what could be improved.

Continuous Learning: Allocate time for learning and improving your trading skills. This might include reading trading books, attending webinars, or following market news.

Example: A trader might start their day by reviewing overnight market news, analyzing key technical indicators, and identifying potential trading opportunities. At the end of the day, they review their trades and make notes for improvement.

5. CONTINGENCY PLANS

Contingency plans are strategies for responding to unexpected market events or changes in your trading performance. They help you stay prepared and make informed decisions under various market conditions.

Key Components:

Unexpected Market Events: Plan how you will respond to major news events, economic releases, or market disruptions that could impact your trading strategy.

Performance Issues: Develop a plan for addressing periods of underperformance or significant losses. This might include pausing trading, reassessing your strategy, or adjusting your risk management rules.

Technical Problems: Consider how you will handle technical issues such as internet outages, platform failures, or other disruptions that could impact your ability to trade.

Example: A trader might have a contingency plan to stop trading for a day if their account experiences a loss of 5% or more. They would then review their strategy and make necessary adjustments before resuming trading.

THE IMPORTANCE OF A TRADING PLAN

Staying Disciplined: A trading plan helps you maintain discipline by providing a clear set of rules and guidelines for your trading activities. It prevents impulsive decisions driven by emotions, ensuring that your actions are based on a well-thought-out strategy.

Tip: Keep your trading plan easily accessible and refer to it regularly to stay on track and maintain discipline.

Setting Clear Objectives: A trading plan includes clear, measurable objectives that guide your trading activities. These objectives help you stay focused and provide a benchmark for evaluating your progress over time.

Tip: Define both short-term and long-term goals in your trading plan. For example, your short-term goal might be to achieve a certain percentage return each month, while your long-term goal could be to build a diversified trading portfolio.

Managing Risk: Risk management is a critical component of any trading plan. By setting parameters for risk management, such as position sizing and stop-loss orders, your plan helps protect your capital and minimize potential losses.

Tip: Include specific risk management rules in your trading plan. For example, limit the amount of capital you're willing to risk on a single trade to no more than 2% of your total trading account.

COMPONENTS OF A TRADING PLAN

Defining Your Trading Strategy: Your trading strategy is the foundation of your trading plan. It outlines the methods and criteria you will use to identify trading opportunities, enter and exit trades, and manage your positions. Your strategy should be based on a thorough analysis of the market and aligned with your financial goals and risk tolerance.

Tip: Be as detailed as possible when defining your trading strategy. Include specific criteria for entering and exiting trades, as well as any indicators or tools you will rely on.

Establishing Risk Management Rules: Risk management is a crucial aspect of any trading plan. This section should cover how you will manage your risk, including your approach to position sizing, stop-loss orders, and overall exposure. Effective risk management helps protect your capital and ensures that you can continue trading even in the face of losses.

Tip: Consider using a risk-reward ratio to guide your trading decisions. For example, you might aim for a minimum of a 2:1 risk-reward ratio, meaning you seek to gain twice as much as you're willing to risk on any given trade.

Setting Financial Goals: Your financial goals should be realistic and aligned with your overall trading strategy. This section of your plan should specify both short-term and long-term goals, as well as how you plan to achieve them.

Tip: Break down your financial goals into manageable steps. For example, set monthly or quarterly targets that contribute to your long-term objectives.

Outlining Your Trading Routine: Your trading plan should include a daily or weekly routine that outlines when and how you will conduct your trading activities. This routine helps you stay organized and ensures that you are consistently reviewing and analyzing the market.

Tip: Include time for market analysis, strategy review, and performance evaluation in your routine. Consistency is key to successful trading.

Including Contingency Plans: Markets can be unpredictable, so it's essential to have contingency plans in place. This section should outline how you will respond to unexpected market events or significant changes in your trading performance.

Tip: Consider what actions you will take if your strategy underperforms, such as pausing trading to reassess or adjusting your risk management rules.

DEVELOPING YOUR TRADING PLAN

Start with a Template: If you're new to trading, starting with a basic trading plan template can be helpful (downloadable in a spreadsheet format). As you gain experience, you can customize and expand your plan to better suit your needs.

Trading Month	Trading Day	Daily $ Gain	Realized Balance	Gain % From Start
		Daily Pips Target	15	
		Daily % Gain	1.50%	
		Start Balance	£1,000.00	
M1	0	0	£1,000.00	0.00%
	1	£15.00	£1,015.00	1.50%
	2	£15.23	£1,030.23	3.02%
	3	£15.45	£1,045.68	4.57%
	4	£15.69	£1,061.36	6.14%
	5	£15.92	£1,077.28	7.73%
	6	£16.16	£1,093.44	9.34%
	7	£16.40	£1,109.84	10.98%
	8	£16.65	£1,126.49	12.65%
	9	£16.90	£1,143.39	14.34%
	10	£17.15	£1,160.54	16.05%
	11	£17.41	£1,177.95	17.79%
	12	£17.67	£1,195.62	19.56%
	13	£17.93	£1,213.55	21.36%
	14	£18.20	£1,231.76	23.18%
	15	£18.48	£1,250.23	25.02%

A sample Trading Plan template

Tip: Look for trading plan templates online that align with your trading style and objectives. Modify them as needed to fit your specific situation.

Personalizing Your Plan: Your trading plan should reflect your personal trading style, risk tolerance, and financial goals. Take the time to tailor each section of the plan to suit your individual needs and preferences.

Tip: Be honest with yourself about your strengths, weaknesses, and risk tolerance. Your trading plan should be realistic and achievable based on your unique circumstances.

Testing and Refining Your Plan: Before implementing your trading plan in a live market, it's essential to test it through backtesting and demo trading. This allows you to refine your plan based on real-world data and performance.

Tip: Regularly review and adjust your trading plan as needed. Markets evolve, and so should your plan. Continuously seek ways to improve and adapt your strategy.

ADHERING TO YOUR TRADING PLAN

Avoiding Emotional Trading: One of the main benefits of a trading plan is that it helps you avoid emotional trading. By sticking to your plan, you can prevent decisions based on fear, greed, or impulse.

Tip: If you find yourself tempted to deviate from your plan, take a step back and remind yourself of your long-term goals. Discipline is key to trading success.

Regular Performance Reviews: Regularly reviewing your performance against your trading plan helps you stay accountable and ensures that your strategy remains effective. Use these reviews to make necessary adjustments and stay on track.

Tip: Set aside time at the end of each trading week or month to review your trades, assess your progress toward your goals, and make any necessary changes to your plan.

Continuous Learning and Adaptation: The market is constantly changing, and so should your trading plan. Continuous learning and adaptation are essential for staying ahead in the trading game.

Tip: Stay informed about market trends, new strategies, and emerging technologies that could impact your trading. Be willing to adapt your plan as you gain new insights and experience.

Building a trading plan is a critical step in becoming a successful trader. By clearly defining your strategy, risk management rules, and financial goals, you create a roadmap for your trading journey. A well-crafted trading plan provides structure, discipline, and a clear path to achieving your trading objectives. Remember, a trading plan is not static—it should evolve as you gain experience and as market conditions change.

Stay disciplined, adhere to your plan, and continuously seek ways to improve. With a solid trading plan, you'll be better equipped to navigate the natural gas market and achieve your trading goals.

PART 8: RISK MANAGEMENT IN NATURAL GAS TRADING

CHAPTER 29: IDENTIFYING AND MITIGATING RISKS

In the volatile world of natural gas trading, understanding and managing risk is crucial for achieving long-term success. Trading inherently involves various risks, from market fluctuations to operational errors, and effectively identifying and mitigating these risks can help protect your capital and enhance your trading performance. In this chapter, we will explore the different types of risks associated with natural gas trading, methods for identifying these risks, and strategies for mitigating them.

TYPES OF RISKS IN NATURAL GAS TRADING

Natural gas trading exposes traders to several types of risks, each with its own characteristics and implications.

1. MARKET RISK

Market risk, also known as price risk, arises from fluctuations in natural gas prices. This type of risk can affect the value of your trading positions and overall profitability.

Price Volatility: Natural gas prices can be highly volatile due to factors such as supply and demand imbalances, geopolitical events, and weather patterns.

Unexpected Price Movements: Sudden and sharp price movements can lead to significant losses if not managed properly.

2. CREDIT RISK

Credit risk refers to the possibility that a counterparty may default on their financial obligations, impacting your trading positions and overall financial stability.

Counterparty Default: If a counterparty fails to fulfill their contractual obligations, it can result in financial losses.

Settlement Risk: There is a risk that a counterparty may not settle trades or transactions as agreed, leading to potential disputes and financial losses.

3. LIQUIDITY RISK

Liquidity risk involves the difficulty of buying or selling positions without significantly impacting market prices.

Market Depth: In markets with low trading volume or depth, it may be challenging to execute trades at desired prices.

Order Execution: Large orders or positions may affect market prices, leading to slippage and unfavorable execution.

4. OPERATIONAL RISK

Operational risk pertains to the risks associated with trading processes, systems, and human errors.

System Failures: Technical issues, such as trading platform outages or software malfunctions, can disrupt trading activities.

Human Error: Mistakes in trade execution, data entry, or risk management can lead to financial losses.

5. REGULATORY AND COMPLIANCE RISK

Regulatory and compliance risk involves the possibility of legal and regulatory challenges affecting trading activities.

Regulatory Changes: Changes in regulations or compliance requirements can impact trading strategies and operations.

Legal Disputes: Legal issues, such as disputes over contracts or regulatory violations, can lead to financial penalties and reputational damage.

IDENTIFYING RISKS

Identifying risks is the first step in managing them effectively. Here are some methods to help you identify risks in natural gas trading:

1. RISK ASSESSMENT

Conduct a thorough risk assessment to evaluate the potential risks associated with your trading activities.

Scenario Analysis: Analyze different market scenarios and their potential impact on your trading positions. This helps identify vulnerabilities and areas of exposure.

Historical Data Analysis: Review historical data and past performance to understand how similar risks have affected the market and your trades.

2. RISK MONITORING

Implement risk monitoring practices to track and assess risks continuously.

Real-Time Monitoring: Use real-time data and trading tools to monitor market conditions, price movements, and trade execution.

Performance Metrics: Track performance metrics such as drawdowns, volatility, and trading costs to identify potential risks and areas for improvement.

3. RISK REPORTING

Develop a risk reporting system to document and communicate risk-related information.

Risk Reports: Generate regular risk reports that summarize risk exposures, potential impacts, and mitigation strategies.

Communication: Share risk reports with relevant stakeholders, such as trading teams and risk managers, to ensure awareness and alignment.

MITIGATING RISKS

Once risks have been identified, it's important to implement strategies to mitigate them effectively. Here are some key risk mitigation strategies:

1. DIVERSIFICATION

Diversification involves spreading your investments and trades across different assets, strategies, or market conditions to reduce overall risk.

Asset Diversification: Invest in a variety of natural gas-related assets, such as futures contracts, options, and equities, to minimize exposure to any single asset.

Strategy Diversification: Use multiple trading strategies to balance risk and enhance potential returns.

2. RISK MANAGEMENT TECHNIQUES

Implement risk management techniques to protect your capital and manage exposure.

Stop-Loss Orders: Use stop-loss orders to limit potential losses on each trade. Set stop-loss levels based on your risk tolerance and market conditions.

Take-Profit Orders: Set take-profit orders to lock in gains and protect profits from potential reversals.

Position Sizing: Adjust position sizes based on your risk tolerance and trading strategy to avoid excessive exposure.

3. HEDGING

Hedging involves using financial instruments or strategies to offset potential losses from adverse price movements.

Futures Contracts: Use futures contracts to hedge against price fluctuations and manage risk exposure.

Options: Use options contracts to create protective positions and limit potential losses.

4. OPERATIONAL CONTROLS

Implement operational controls to manage risks associated with trading processes and systems.

Technical Infrastructure: Ensure that your trading platform and systems are reliable and secure. Regularly test and update your technology to prevent system failures.

Trade Review Procedures: Establish procedures for reviewing and validating trades to minimize errors and ensure accuracy.

5. COMPLIANCE AND REGULATION

Stay informed about regulatory changes and ensure compliance with legal requirements.

Regulatory Updates: Monitor changes in regulations and compliance requirements to stay aligned with legal standards.

BEST PRACTICES FOR RISK MANAGEMENT

To effectively manage risks in natural gas trading, follow these best practices:

Develop a Risk Management Plan: Create a comprehensive risk management plan that outlines your risk identification, assessment, and mitigation strategies.

Stay Informed: Continuously monitor market conditions, regulatory changes, and technological advancements to stay informed about potential risks.

Regularly Review and Update: Regularly review and update your risk management strategies to adapt to changing market conditions and improve effectiveness.

Educate and Train: Invest in education and training for yourself and your trading team to enhance risk awareness and management skills.

Identifying and mitigating risks is a fundamental aspect of successful natural gas trading. By understanding the different types of risks, implementing effective risk management strategies, and following best practices, traders can protect their capital, enhance their trading performance, and achieve long-term success.

CHAPTER 30: UNDERSTANDING LEVERAGE AND MARGIN

Leverage and margin are critical concepts in trading that can significantly impact your potential returns and risks. They are essential tools for maximizing trading opportunities but must be used carefully to avoid substantial losses. In this chapter, we will explore what leverage and margin are, how they work, and their implications for natural gas trading.

WHAT IS LEVERAGE?

Leverage allows traders to control a large position in the market with a relatively small amount of capital. It amplifies both potential gains and potential losses, making it a powerful but risky tool.

1. HOW LEVERAGE WORKS

Leverage is expressed as a ratio, such as 10:1 or 50:1. This ratio indicates how much larger your trading position is compared to the amount of capital you need to put up. For example, with 10:1 leverage, you can control a $10,000 position with just $1,000 of your own money.

Example: If you use 10:1 leverage to buy a futures contract worth $10,000, you only need $1,000 as margin. If the price moves in your favor, your gains are based on the full $10,000 position, not just your $1,000 investment. Conversely, if the price moves against you, losses are also calculated based on the full position.

2. ADVANTAGES OF LEVERAGE

Increased Buying Power: Leverage allows you to take larger positions with a smaller amount of capital, potentially increasing your returns.

Capital Efficiency: By using leverage, you can allocate your capital to other investments or opportunities while still maintaining a significant position in the market.

3. RISKS OF LEVERAGE

Amplified Losses: Just as leverage can magnify gains, it can also magnify losses. A small adverse price movement can result in significant losses, potentially exceeding your initial margin.

Margin Calls: If your position moves against you and your account equity falls below the required margin level, you may face a margin call. This requires you to deposit additional funds to maintain your position or face liquidation.

WHAT IS MARGIN?

Margin is the amount of money required to open and maintain a leveraged position. It acts as a security deposit to cover potential losses and ensure that you can meet your trading obligations.

1. TYPES OF MARGIN

Initial Margin: This is the amount of money you need to deposit to open a new position. It is a percentage of the total position size and varies depending on the leverage ratio and the asset being traded.

Maintenance Margin: This is the minimum amount of equity required to keep a position open. If your account equity falls below this level due to adverse price movements, you may receive a margin call.

2. MARGIN REQUIREMENTS

Margin requirements are set by brokers and can vary based on market conditions, asset volatility, and the leverage ratio. It's essential to understand these requirements to manage your positions effectively.

Broker Requirements: Different brokers have different margin requirements, so it's crucial to check your broker's specific policies and ensure you meet their criteria.

Market Conditions: Margin requirements can change based on market conditions and volatility. During periods of high volatility, brokers may increase margin requirements to account for increased risk.

MANAGING LEVERAGE AND MARGIN

Effectively managing leverage and margin is vital for maintaining control over your trading risks and capital.

1. ASSESSING YOUR RISK TOLERANCE

Before using leverage, assess your risk tolerance and determine how much risk you are willing to take. Consider factors such as your trading experience, capital size, and market conditions.

Risk Tolerance: Ensure that your use of leverage aligns with your risk tolerance and trading strategy. Avoid using excessive leverage that could lead to substantial losses.

2. SETTING STOP-LOSS ORDERS

Implement stop-loss orders to limit potential losses and protect your capital. Stop-loss orders automatically close a position when the price reaches a specified level, helping you manage risk and avoid significant losses.

Stop-Loss Strategy: Determine appropriate stop-loss levels based on your trading strategy and risk tolerance. Adjust stop-loss orders as needed to reflect changes in market conditions and position size.

3. MONITORING MARGIN LEVELS

Regularly monitor your account margin levels and be prepared to respond to margin calls. Ensure that you have sufficient funds in your account to meet margin requirements and avoid forced liquidation.

Margin Monitoring: Use tools and alerts provided by your broker to track margin levels and receive notifications of potential margin calls.

4. AVOIDING OVERLEVERAGING

Be cautious of overleveraging, where the size of your positions exceeds your ability to manage risk effectively. Overleveraging increases the likelihood of margin calls and significant losses.

Position Sizing: Use appropriate position sizing based on your capital, leverage ratio, and risk management strategy. Avoid taking on more risk than you can afford.

LEVERAGING IN DIFFERENT TRADING SCENARIOS

Leverage and margin can have different implications depending on the type of trading you are engaged in. Here's how they apply to various trading scenarios:

1. FUTURES TRADING

In futures trading, leverage is commonly used to control large positions with a relatively small margin. Understanding margin requirements and managing leverage is crucial for successful futures trading.

Futures Contracts: Leverage allows traders to control large futures contracts with a smaller margin, but it also requires careful management to avoid excessive risk.

2. OPTIONS TRADING

Options trading involves leveraging through the use of options contracts, which can amplify potential returns and losses. Margin requirements for options may vary based on the type of options and trading strategy.

Options Positions: Manage leverage and margin based on the type of options strategies used, such as covered calls or naked puts, and ensure you understand the associated risks.

3. CFD TRADING

Contracts for Difference (CFDs) are another leveraged trading instrument that allows traders to speculate on price movements without owning the underlying asset. Margin requirements for CFDs can vary based on the asset and broker.

CFD Leverage: Use leverage in CFD trading cautiously, considering the potential for significant gains and losses. Monitor margin levels and adjust positions as needed.

Understanding leverage and margin is essential for navigating the complexities of natural gas trading. Leverage amplifies both potential gains and losses, while margin acts as a security deposit for maintaining leveraged positions. By assessing your risk tolerance, setting stop-loss orders, monitoring margin levels, and avoiding overleveraging, you can manage leverage and margin effectively and protect your capital.

CHAPTER 31: THE IMPORTANCE OF STOP-LOSS ORDERS

Stop-loss orders are fundamental tools in trading that help manage risk and protect capital. They are designed to limit potential losses by automatically closing a position when the market reaches a predetermined price level. In this chapter, we will explore what stop-loss orders are, their types, their role in risk management, and best practices for effectively using them.

WHAT IS A STOP-LOSS ORDER?

A stop-loss order is a type of order placed with a broker to sell a security when it reaches a specific price, known as the **stop price**. The primary purpose of a stop-loss order is to limit potential losses on a trade by exiting the position before losses escalate further. This tool is a cornerstone of risk management, ensuring that traders can cap their losses and protect their capital.

How Stop-Loss Orders Work

Stop-loss orders are designed to automatically sell a security when it falls to a predetermined price. When the market price of a security reaches this stop price, the stop-loss order is activated and becomes a market order. This transition means that the order will be executed at the best available price once the stop price is hit, which may differ from the stop price due to market fluctuations.

Example: Suppose you buy a natural gas futures contract at $3.00 per MMBtu and set a stop-loss order at $2.80. If the price falls to $2.80, the stop-loss order will be triggered, converting it into a market order, and your position will be sold at the current market price. This mechanism helps to ensure that you exit the trade and limit your losses if the market moves against your position.

TYPES OF STOP-LOSS ORDERS

There are several types of stop-loss orders, each with its characteristics and specific uses. Understanding these differences can help you select the best type for your trading strategy.

1. STANDARD STOP-LOSS ORDER

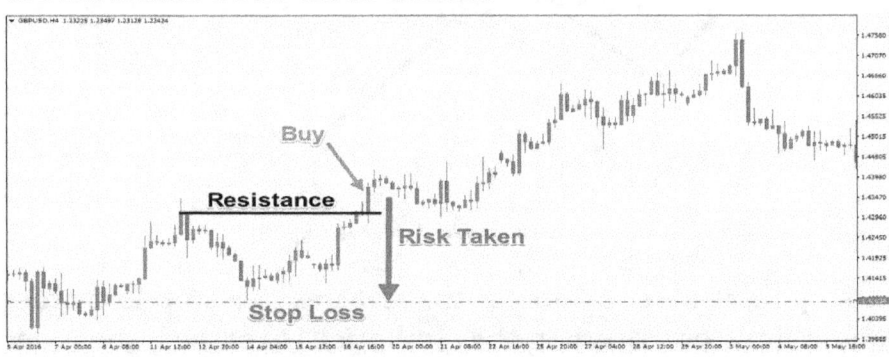

A Standard Stop-Loss Order: forextraininggroup.com

A standard stop-loss order becomes a market order once the stop price is reached. This order aims to exit the position quickly to minimize losses, but the execution price might slightly differ from the stop price due to the market's liquidity and volatility.

Advantages:

Simplicity: Easy to understand and implement, making it a popular choice for many traders.

Speed: Ensures that the position is closed promptly when the stop price is reached, which is critical in fast-moving markets.

Disadvantages:

Price Variability: In volatile markets, the execution price may differ from the stop price, leading to a higher loss than anticipated.

Market Gaps: If the market opens significantly lower than the stop price (a gap down), the order might be executed at a much lower price.

2. STOP-LIMIT ORDER

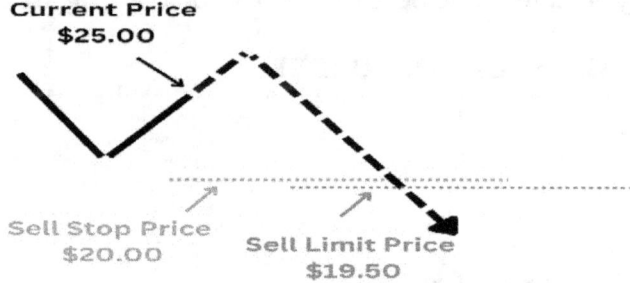

A Stop-Limit Order: learn.bybit.com

A stop-limit order combines the features of a stop-loss order and a limit order. When the stop price is reached, the order becomes a limit order, which will only be executed at the limit price or better. This type of order gives traders more control over the execution price.

Advantages:

Price Control: Provides a guaranteed minimum execution price, reducing the risk of executing at an unfavorable price.

Flexibility: Allows traders to set specific limits based on their analysis and market expectations.

Disadvantages:

Execution Risk: If the market price moves quickly away from the limit price, the order may not be executed at all, leaving the position open and exposed to further losses.

Complexity: Requires careful setting of both stop and limit prices to balance risk and reward effectively.

3. TRAILING STOP ORDER

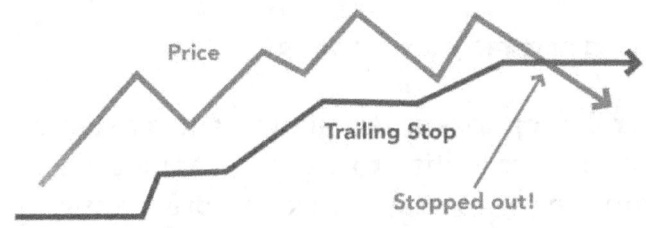

A Trailing Stop Order: investinganswers.com

A trailing stop order is a dynamic stop-loss order that automatically adjusts the stop price as the market price moves in the trader's favor. The stop price trails the market price by a specified amount or percentage, allowing traders to lock in profits while protecting against significant losses if the price reverses.

Advantages:

Profit Protection: As the market price rises, the trailing stop adjusts upwards, locking in profits.

Loss Limitation: If the price drops, the trailing stop prevents further losses by selling the security at the set stop price.

Disadvantages:

Premature Exits: The stop price may be triggered during normal market fluctuations, potentially leading to exits that are too early.

Complex Setup: Determining the appropriate trailing distance requires careful consideration of market volatility and trading objectives.

THE ROLE OF STOP-LOSS ORDERS IN RISK MANAGEMENT

Stop-loss orders are a critical component of effective risk management, providing several key benefits that help traders manage their trading strategies and protect their capital.

1. LIMITING POTENTIAL LOSSES

Risk Control: Stop-loss orders allow traders to define the maximum loss they are willing to accept on a trade, helping to control the amount of capital at risk and preventing losses from spiraling out of control.

Predetermined Limits: By setting a stop price, traders can establish clear boundaries for their losses, ensuring that their risk exposure aligns with their overall trading strategy and risk tolerance.

2. MAINTAINING DISCIPLINE

Emotional Control: Trading can be emotionally challenging, and it is easy to let emotions dictate decisions. Stop-loss orders enforce discipline by ensuring that trades are exited based on predefined criteria rather than emotions or reactive decisions.

Preventing Emotional Decision-Making: By automating the exit strategy, stop-loss orders help traders avoid the temptation to hold onto losing positions in the hope that the market will reverse.

3. PROTECTING CAPITAL

Capital Preservation: Stop-loss orders are essential for preserving trading capital by automatically closing positions before losses accumulate, helping to maintain the overall value of the trading portfolio.

Long-Term Success: Protecting capital ensures that traders have the financial resources to continue trading and achieve their long-term financial goals. Successful trading is not just about making profits but also about minimizing losses.

BEST PRACTICES FOR USING STOP-LOSS ORDERS

To effectively use stop-loss orders and maximize their benefits, consider the following best practices:

1. SETTING APPROPRIATE STOP PRICES

Technical Analysis: Utilize technical analysis tools such as support and resistance levels, trendlines, and other indicators to set stop prices that align with market dynamics. This approach helps ensure that stop prices are based on objective market factors rather than arbitrary levels.

Volatility Considerations: Adjust stop prices according to market volatility. In highly volatile markets, setting stop prices too close to the entry price can result in frequent stop-outs due to normal market fluctuations.

2. AVOIDING COMMON MISTAKES

Over-Narrowing: Setting stop prices too close to the entry price may lead to frequent triggering of stop-loss orders, resulting in unnecessary losses. It's important to balance the need for risk protection with the potential for market fluctuations.

Ignoring Market Conditions: Failing to account for market volatility or changing conditions can lead to ineffective stop-loss orders. Regularly review and adjust stop prices based on current market conditions.

3. REGULARLY REVIEWING AND ADJUSTING

Trade Review: Periodically assess the effectiveness of your stop-loss orders. Review past trades to determine if stop-loss orders were appropriately set and executed, and make adjustments as needed to align with your trading strategy.

Market Changes: Regularly review and adjust your stop-loss orders based on changes in market conditions, trade performance, and evolving risk management needs. This proactive approach helps ensure that your risk management strategy remains effective over time.

4. COMBINING WITH OTHER RISK MANAGEMENT TOOLS

Position Sizing: Combine stop-loss orders with appropriate position sizing to manage risk and exposure effectively. By limiting the size of your positions, you can further reduce the potential impact of losses on your overall portfolio.

Diversification: Use stop-loss orders in conjunction with diversification strategies to spread risk across different assets and trades. Diversification helps protect your portfolio from significant losses in any single trade or market.

5. UTILIZING TECHNOLOGY AND AUTOMATION

Trading Platforms: Leverage the capabilities of modern trading platforms to set and manage stop-loss orders efficiently. Many platforms offer advanced features such as conditional orders and automated trading strategies that can enhance the effectiveness of stop-loss orders.

Automated Strategies: Consider incorporating automated trading strategies that include stop-loss orders as part of your overall trading plan. Automated strategies can help reduce the risk of human error and ensure that stop-loss orders are executed consistently.

Stop-loss orders are essential tools for managing risk and protecting capital in natural gas trading. By setting predefined exit points, traders can limit potential losses, maintain discipline, and preserve capital. Understanding the different types of stop-loss orders, their role in risk management, and best practices for their use is crucial for successful trading.

CHAPTER 32: DIVERSIFICATION STRATEGIES

Diversification is a fundamental strategy in trading and investing that involves spreading your investments across different assets, instruments, or markets to reduce risk and enhance potential returns. In the context of natural gas trading, diversification can help manage risk, optimize returns, and improve overall portfolio performance by mitigating the impact of market volatility and specific risks associated with trading natural gas.

This chapter explores the concept of diversification, various diversification strategies, and their application in natural gas trading, specifically through online brokers.

WHAT IS DIVERSIFICATION?

Diversification involves allocating investments across a range of assets or positions to minimize the impact of any single asset's poor performance on the overall portfolio. The goal is to achieve a more stable and consistent performance by reducing exposure to individual risks and smoothing out the volatility that can occur in any one area of the market.

1. BENEFITS OF DIVERSIFICATION

Risk Reduction: By spreading investments across various assets and strategies, diversification reduces the impact of adverse movements in any single asset or market, thereby lowering overall portfolio risk.

Smoother Returns: Diversified portfolios often experience less volatility and more stable returns compared to concentrated portfolios that are heavily weighted in one type of asset or market.

Improved Opportunities: Diversification allows you to tap into various markets or asset classes, potentially enhancing overall returns by taking advantage of different market cycles and trends.

TYPES OF DIVERSIFICATION

Diversification can be implemented across several dimensions in natural gas trading, including asset diversification, geographic diversification, and sector diversification.

Asset Diversification: Asset diversification involves investing in different types of assets, such as stocks, bonds, commodities, and real estate, to reduce the risk associated with any single asset class. In natural gas trading, this means combining natural gas with other energy commodities or financial instruments.

Geographic Diversification: Geographic diversification entails investing in markets across different regions or countries to spread risk across various economic environments and political landscapes. This strategy can be particularly relevant for traders who access multiple exchanges and international markets through online brokers.

Sector Diversification: Sector diversification means investing in different sectors or industries to reduce exposure to sector-specific risks. For natural gas traders, this might involve trading across different segments of the energy market, including crude oil, propane, and other related commodities.

DIVERSIFICATION STRATEGIES IN NATURAL GAS TRADING

In natural gas trading, diversification strategies can be applied across different instruments, markets, and trading approaches to manage risk and optimize returns. Here are some specific strategies you can employ:

1. INSTRUMENT DIVERSIFICATION

Futures Contracts: Diversify your trading activities by trading various natural gas futures contracts with different expiration dates and contract sizes. This approach helps to spread risk across different time horizons and market conditions.

Options Contracts: Utilize options contracts to gain exposure to natural gas prices with different strike prices and expiration dates. Options can provide flexibility and additional strategies such as straddles or strangles, allowing traders to hedge or speculate on price movements.

CFDs (Contracts for Difference): Trade CFDs to speculate on natural gas price movements without owning the underlying asset. CFDs offer leverage and flexibility, allowing traders to take both long and short positions.

2. MARKET DIVERSIFICATION

Different Exchanges: Trade natural gas on multiple exchanges, such as the New York Mercantile Exchange (NYMEX), Intercontinental Exchange (ICE), or other international exchanges. Each exchange may offer different contract specifications, liquidity levels, and trading hours, providing various opportunities and challenges.

Related Commodities: Invest in related commodities, such as crude oil, propane, or electricity, which may have correlated price movements with natural gas. This strategy can help to capitalize on the relationships between different energy markets.

3. TRADING STRATEGY DIVERSIFICATION

Technical Analysis: Use technical indicators, chart patterns, and trend analysis to guide trading decisions. Diversify your technical strategies by using a mix of short-term and long-term indicators or by combining different technical approaches.

Fundamental Analysis: Incorporate fundamental analysis by evaluating supply and demand factors, economic indicators, and market conditions. Diversify your analysis by considering a range of fundamental factors such as weather patterns, geopolitical events, and industry trends.

Quantitative Models: Utilize quantitative models and algorithmic trading strategies to make data-driven trading decisions. Diversify your quantitative strategies by exploring different models and algorithms that focus on various aspects of market behavior.

IMPLEMENTING DIVERSIFICATION IN NATURAL GAS TRADING

To effectively implement diversification in natural gas trading, consider the following steps:

1. ASSESSING RISK TOLERANCE

Risk Assessment: Evaluate your risk tolerance and investment objectives to determine the appropriate level of diversification for your trading portfolio. Consider factors such as capital size, trading experience, and market conditions when assessing risk tolerance.

Investment Goals: Align your diversification strategies with your overall investment goals and trading objectives. Clearly define your goals to ensure that your diversification efforts support your long-term success.

2. ALLOCATING CAPITAL

Capital Allocation: Allocate capital across different instruments, markets, and strategies based on your diversification plan. Ensure that your capital allocation reflects your risk tolerance and trading goals.

Portfolio Balance: Strive for a balanced portfolio that includes a mix of different assets and strategies. Regularly review and adjust your capital allocation to maintain this balance as market conditions and your investment goals evolve.

3. MONITORING AND ADJUSTING

Performance Review: Regularly monitor your diversified portfolio and make adjustments as needed to maintain alignment with your risk tolerance and objectives. Track the performance of your diversified assets and strategies to evaluate their effectiveness.

Rebalancing: Adjust your capital allocation and diversification strategies based on changes in market conditions, performance, and risk exposure. Rebalancing your portfolio ensures that you remain aligned with your investment goals and risk tolerance.

4. COMBINING DIVERSIFICATION WITH OTHER RISK MANAGEMENT TOOLS

Stop-Loss Orders: Use stop-loss orders to limit losses and protect individual positions within your diversified portfolio. Stop-loss orders can help to manage risk by automatically closing positions that reach a predetermined loss threshold.

Hedging: Employ hedging strategies to manage risk and protect against adverse price movements in your diversified assets. Hedging can involve using options, futures, or other financial instruments to offset potential losses in your primary positions.

EXAMPLES OF DIVERSIFICATION IN PRACTICE

Here are a few examples of how diversification can be applied in natural gas trading:

Example 1: Diversifying Across Futures Contracts

A trader may choose to diversify their exposure to natural gas by trading futures contracts with different expiration dates. For instance, they might hold positions in both the near-month and far-month futures contracts to balance exposure to short-term and long-term price movements. This approach helps to mitigate the risk of adverse price movements in any one contract month.

Example 2: Combining Technical and Fundamental Strategies

A trader may use both technical analysis and fundamental analysis in their trading approach. For example, they might use technical indicators to time entries and exits while also considering fundamental factors such as supply reports and weather forecasts. This strategy diversifies their decision-making process and enhances their ability to adapt to changing market conditions.

Example 3: Investing in Related Commodities

A trader may diversify by investing in related commodities, such as crude oil or propane, which have price correlations with natural gas. This approach can help manage risk and capitalize on related market movements. For example, if natural gas prices are expected to rise due to increased demand, the trader might also consider long positions in propane or crude oil.

Diversification is a powerful strategy for managing risk and optimizing returns in natural gas trading. By spreading investments across different instruments, markets, and strategies, traders can reduce exposure to individual risks, achieve more stable returns, and enhance overall portfolio performance.

PART 9: TOOLS AND PLATFORMS FOR NATURAL GAS TRADING

CHAPTER 33: SELECTING A TRADING PLATFORM

Selecting the right trading platform is one of the most crucial decisions you'll make as a natural gas trader. A trading platform is more than just software; it's your gateway to the markets, your tool for executing trades, analyzing market data, and managing your trading activities. The choice of platform can significantly impact your trading experience, efficiency, and ultimately your success in the natural gas market.

In this chapter, we will delve into the key factors to consider when selecting a trading platform, evaluate various platform features, and provide guidance on making an informed decision that aligns with your trading goals.

SELECTING A TRADING PLATFORM:

Choosing the right trading platform is crucial for your trading experience and success. There are several types of platforms available, each with its own set of features and benefits.

CHAPTER 33: SELECTING A TRADING PLATFORM | 225

MT4 / MT5 Trading Platform: cmcmarkets.com

Desktop Platforms: These are downloadable applications that you install on your computer. They often offer the most comprehensive set of features, including advanced charting tools, custom indicators, and automated trading capabilities. Examples include MetaTrader 4 (MT4) and MetaTrader 5 (MT5).

MT4 / MT5 Trading Platform: cmcmarkets.com

Web-Based Platforms: These platforms can be accessed through your internet browser without the need for installation. They offer the convenience of trading from any computer with internet access and are generally user-friendly. Examples include TradingView and cTrader.

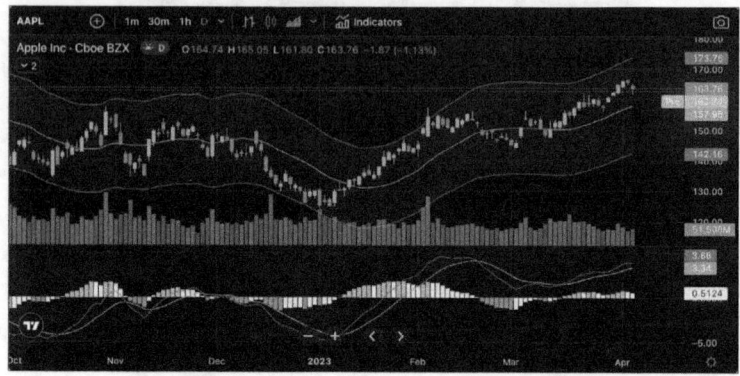

TradingView Desktop Application: tradingview.com

Mobile Platforms: Designed for smartphones and tablets, these platforms allow you to trade on the go. They are ideal for traders who need to monitor and manage their trades from anywhere. Most major trading platforms offer mobile versions, such as MT4 and MT5 mobile apps.

KEY FACTORS TO CONSIDER

When choosing a trading platform for natural gas trading, several critical factors should guide your decision. These factors not only affect your day-to-day trading activities but also your long-term success and satisfaction with the platform.

1. USER INTERFACE AND EXPERIENCE

The user interface (UI) and overall user experience (UX) of a trading platform are fundamental to how effectively you can navigate the platform, execute trades, and manage your portfolio.

Ease of Use: The platform should have an intuitive and user-friendly interface. Whether you're a novice or an experienced trader, the platform should be easy to navigate, with clear labeling and logical layouts. A steep learning curve can hinder your trading efficiency, especially during fast-moving markets where every second counts.

Customization: Evaluate the platform's ability to customize layouts, charts, and trading tools according to your preferences. A customizable interface allows you to arrange the tools and information you need most frequently, enhancing your efficiency and focus during trading sessions. This includes the ability to save custom chart setups, create personalized watchlists, and adjust the layout of trading dashboards.

2. TRADING TOOLS AND FEATURES

A robust trading platform should offer a comprehensive set of tools and features that support your trading strategies and decision-making process, particularly in a dynamic market like natural gas.

Charting Tools: Ensure the platform provides advanced charting capabilities, including multiple timeframes, a wide range of technical indicators, and drawing tools. This is essential for analyzing price movements and identifying trading opportunities. Look for platforms that allow you to apply and customize indicators like moving averages, RSI, Bollinger Bands, and others crucial to your strategy.

Order Types: Verify that the platform supports various order types, such as market orders, limit orders, stop orders, and trailing stops. This flexibility allows you to execute trades according to your specific strategies, whether you're day trading, swing trading, or hedging positions.

News and Analysis: Access to real-time news, market analysis, and economic calendars is vital for staying informed about market developments that can impact natural gas prices. The platform should integrate reliable news sources and offer in-depth analysis, allowing you to make informed trading decisions based on current market conditions.

3. PERFORMANCE AND RELIABILITY

The performance and reliability of a trading platform are critical for ensuring smooth and efficient trading operations. In volatile markets like natural gas, where prices can change rapidly, the platform's performance can make a significant difference.

Speed and Execution: Choose a platform known for fast order execution and minimal latency. Delays in order execution can lead to slippage, where your trade is executed at a different price than expected, potentially impacting your profitability. The platform should execute your orders swiftly, ensuring that your trades are placed at the desired prices.

Uptime and Stability: Opt for a platform with high uptime and stability, particularly during peak trading hours. Downtime or platform instability can prevent you from entering or exiting trades at critical moments, leading to missed opportunities or losses. A reliable platform ensures that you can trade consistently without unexpected disruptions.

4. SECURITY AND SUPPORT

Security and customer support are essential considerations for protecting your trading account and ensuring that you can quickly resolve any issues that arise.

Security Measures: Look for platforms with robust security measures, such as encryption, two-factor authentication (2FA), and secure data storage. These features protect your personal and financial information from unauthorized access, ensuring that your account remains secure.

Customer Support: Assess the quality of customer support provided by the platform, including availability, responsiveness, and the range of support channels (e.g., phone, email, live chat). Effective customer support is crucial for resolving technical issues, answering queries, and providing guidance when you encounter problems. Ideally, support should be available 24/7, particularly during market hours.

5. COSTS AND FEES

Understanding the costs and fees associated with a trading platform is important for managing trading expenses and maximizing profitability. Trading costs can vary widely between platforms and can have a significant impact on your bottom line.

Commission Fees: Review the commission fees for executing trades, including any per-trade or per-contract charges. Some platforms offer commission-free trading, while others charge a fee for each trade. Consider how these fees will affect your trading strategy, especially if you trade frequently or in high volumes.

Spreads and Slippage: Consider the spreads (the difference between the bid and ask prices) and potential slippage (the difference between the expected price and the executed price) that may affect your trading costs. Tight spreads and low slippage are crucial for minimizing costs, particularly in a market as liquid as natural gas.

Account Fees: Check for any account maintenance fees, inactivity fees, or withdrawal fees that may apply. These additional fees can add up over time, reducing your overall profitability, especially if you maintain multiple accounts or trade across various markets.

EVALUATING PLATFORM FEATURES

Different trading platforms offer varying features and functionalities. Here's how to evaluate these features to find the best platform for your needs, particularly in the context of natural gas trading.

1. TRADING INTERFACE

The trading interface is where you'll spend most of your time, so it should be efficient, intuitive, and suited to your trading style.

Order Entry: Evaluate how easy it is to place, modify, and cancel orders using the platform's interface. The process should be straightforward, with minimal clicks or steps required to execute a trade. Look for features like one-click trading or hotkeys, which can speed up the process during fast-moving markets.

Order Management: Look for features that help manage and track open orders, pending orders, and order history. Effective order management tools allow you to monitor your positions in real-time, making it easier to manage risk and ensure that your trades are executed as planned.

2. ANALYTICAL TOOLS

The analytical tools available on the platform should support your trading strategies and decision-making, particularly when trading a volatile commodity like natural gas.

Technical Analysis: Ensure the platform offers a wide range of technical indicators, chart patterns, and drawing tools for technical analysis. Advanced features like backtesting, where you can test your trading strategies against historical data, can also be invaluable for refining your approach.

Fundamental Analysis: Look for tools that provide access to economic data, earnings reports, and other fundamental information relevant to natural gas trading. The ability to integrate fundamental data with technical analysis can give you a more comprehensive view of the market and enhance your trading decisions.

3. MOBILE AND WEB ACCESS

Consider whether the platform offers mobile and web access, enabling you to trade on the go and manage your account from different devices.

Mobile App: Check if the platform has a mobile app with features similar to the desktop version, allowing you to trade and manage your account on smartphones and tablets. A well-designed mobile app should offer full functionality, including charting, order entry, and account management, ensuring that you can trade efficiently even when away from your computer.

Web Access: Ensure the platform provides a web-based version for trading from any device with internet access. This flexibility allows you to log in and trade from anywhere, without needing to install software on every device you use.

4. INTEGRATION AND COMPATIBILITY

Evaluate the platform's integration with other tools and services that you use for trading and analysis.

API Access: If you use automated trading systems or algorithms, check for API access that allows integration with your trading strategies. An open API enables you to connect your own trading bots, scripts, or third-party software to the platform, enhancing your ability to execute complex strategies.

Third-Party Tools: Consider compatibility with third-party tools for additional analysis, research, or trading enhancements. For example, some platforms integrate with external analytics software, news feeds, or social trading networks, allowing you to leverage additional resources and community insights.

MAKING AN INFORMED DECISION

To make an informed decision when selecting a trading platform, follow these steps:

1. RESEARCH AND COMPARE

Conduct thorough research and compare multiple trading platforms based on your criteria and preferences.

Platform Reviews: Read reviews and testimonials from other traders to gain insights into the platform's strengths and weaknesses. Pay attention to feedback regarding ease of use, customer support, and performance, as these factors often vary significantly between platforms.

Feature Comparison: Create a comparison chart of different platforms to evaluate their features, costs, and performance. Consider creating a weighted scoring system that reflects the importance of each factor to your trading style and needs.

2. TEST WITH A DEMO ACCOUNT

Many trading platforms offer demo accounts that allow you to test the platform's features and functionalities without risking real money.

Demo Account: Open a demo account to practice trading, explore the platform's interface, and assess its suitability for your needs. Use this opportunity to test the platform's order execution, charting tools, and any specific features that are important to your trading strategy.

3. CONSIDER CUSTOMER SUPPORT AND EDUCATION

Assess the quality of customer support and educational resources provided by the platform. These resources are essential for resolving issues quickly, improving trading skills, and staying updated with market developments.

Support Services: Look for platforms offering comprehensive support services available 24/7 or during extended hours. Ensure that multiple support channels such as phone, email, and live chat are available, and test the responsiveness of the support team. Efficient customer support can help resolve technical issues and clarify platform features.

Educational Resources: Choose platforms that offer a variety of educational materials like webinars, tutorials, and guides on topics relevant to natural gas trading. Consider interactive features such as demo accounts and quizzes to enhance your learning experience and trading skills.

Community and Networking: Platforms that provide access to trading communities or forums can offer valuable support and insights. Engaging with other traders allows you to share experiences and ideas, helping you refine your trading approach and stay motivated.

Updates and Enhancements: Ensure that the platform regularly updates its features based on user feedback. A commitment to continuous improvement ensures the platform meets evolving trader needs and provides training resources to help you adapt to changes.

Selecting the right trading platform is a vital step for success in natural gas trading. Your choice can greatly impact your trading efficiency and profitability. By considering factors such as user interface, trading tools, performance, security, costs, customer support, and educational resources, you can find a platform that aligns with your trading needs and goals.

Conduct thorough research and test multiple platforms with demo accounts to ensure they suit your trading style. Focus on the quality of customer support and the availability of educational resources to navigate the markets effectively.

The right trading platform will enhance your experience, support your strategies, and contribute to your success in the natural gas market. As you develop your trading skills and adapt to changing market conditions, your chosen platform will be an invaluable tool in achieving your trading objectives.

CHAPTER 34: USING TRADING SOFTWARE AND TOOLS

Trading software and tools are essential for modern trading, providing traders with the means to analyze markets, execute trades, and manage their portfolios efficiently. In this chapter, we will explore various types of trading software and tools, their functionalities, and how to effectively use them to enhance your natural gas trading strategy.

TYPES OF TRADING SOFTWARE AND TOOLS

Trading software and tools come in various forms, each serving different purposes in the trading process. Here's an overview of the key types:

1. CHARTING SOFTWARE

Charting software is a fundamental tool that allows traders to create and analyze price charts for various financial instruments, including natural gas. This software provides visual representations of price movements, making it easier for traders to understand market trends and patterns.

Features: Charting software typically includes interactive charts that can be customized based on time frames and data types. It offers a wide range of technical indicators, such as moving averages, Relative Strength Index (RSI), and Moving Average Convergence Divergence (MACD), which help in analyzing market trends. Additionally, charting software provides drawing tools like trendlines and Fibonacci retracements to highlight specific market movements and key price levels.

Benefits: By using charting software, traders can quickly identify trends, patterns, and key support and resistance levels, which are critical for making informed trading decisions. It enables traders to visualize market dynamics and develop strategies based on historical data and technical analysis.

2. TRADING PLATFORMS

Trading platforms are comprehensive software applications that facilitate the execution of trades, order management, and account monitoring. They act as the primary interface between traders and financial markets.

Features: A robust trading platform includes features such as order execution, trade management, account tracking, real-time quotes, and access to various trading instruments. It may also provide tools for monitoring open positions, managing orders, and viewing historical trading data.

Benefits: Trading platforms offer a centralized interface for managing all aspects of trading, allowing traders to place orders, track their portfolios, and access market data from a single platform. This integration of functionalities simplifies the trading process and enhances efficiency.

3. ANALYTICAL TOOLS

Analytical tools are designed to help traders evaluate market conditions, perform fundamental analysis, and generate trading insights. These tools provide valuable information that aids in decision-making and strategy development.

Features: Analytical tools may include economic calendars that list upcoming events, news feeds that provide real-time updates, sentiment analysis tools that gauge market sentiment, and financial ratios that assess the health of companies and markets.

Benefits: By leveraging analytical tools, traders can stay informed about market events and economic indicators that may impact natural gas prices. This information is crucial for making data-driven trading decisions and adapting to changing market conditions.

4. ALGORITHMIC TRADING SOFTWARE

Algorithmic trading software automates trading strategies by executing trades based on pre-defined rules and algorithms. It enables traders to implement complex strategies without manual intervention.

Features: This type of software includes backtesting capabilities that allow traders to test their strategies using historical data, strategy optimization tools to fine-tune algorithms, automated trade execution features, and risk management functionalities to control exposure.

Benefits: Algorithmic trading software enhances trading efficiency by executing trades based on quantitative models, reducing the potential for human error, and enabling traders to capitalize on market opportunities around the clock.

5. RISK MANAGEMENT TOOLS

Risk management tools assist traders in monitoring and controlling trading risk, helping to protect capital and manage exposure. These tools are essential for maintaining a disciplined trading approach and ensuring long-term success.

Features: Risk management tools may include stop-loss orders that limit potential losses, take-profit orders that secure profits, position sizing calculators that determine the appropriate trade size, and portfolio risk analysis tools that assess overall risk exposure.

Benefits: By using risk management tools, traders can mitigate potential losses and ensure that their trading activities align with their risk management objectives. These tools provide a framework for maintaining a balanced and controlled approach to trading.

HOW TO USE TRADING SOFTWARE AND TOOLS EFFECTIVELY

To maximize the benefits of trading software and tools, follow these guidelines:

1. FAMILIARIZE YOURSELF WITH THE SOFTWARE

Take the time to learn how to use the trading software and tools you choose. A thorough understanding of the software's functionalities is essential for effective use.

Training and Tutorials: Utilize available training resources, tutorials, and documentation to understand the software's capabilities and features. Many platforms offer online courses and video tutorials to help users get started.

Practice: Use demo accounts or practice modes to get hands-on experience with the software before trading with real money. This allows you to explore different features and test your strategies in a risk-free environment.

2. INTEGRATE TOOLS INTO YOUR TRADING STRATEGY

Incorporate trading tools into your trading strategy to enhance decision-making and execution. The right combination of tools can provide a comprehensive view of the market and support your trading objectives.

Technical Analysis: Use charting software to apply technical indicators and identify trading signals based on price patterns and trends. Technical analysis helps traders understand market dynamics and predict future price movements.

Fundamental Analysis: Leverage analytical tools to stay informed about economic events, news, and data releases that impact natural gas prices. Fundamental analysis provides insights into market conditions and helps traders make informed decisions.

3. MONITOR AND ADJUST SETTINGS

Regularly monitor and adjust the settings of your trading software to align with changing market conditions and personal preferences. Customization and flexibility are key to adapting to different trading environments.

Customization: Adjust chart settings, indicator parameters, and risk management tools based on your trading style and market conditions. Tailoring the software to your specific needs can enhance its effectiveness.

Updates: Keep your software up to date with the latest versions and features to ensure optimal performance and security. Regular updates often include bug fixes, security enhancements, and new functionalities.

4. UTILIZE AUTOMATION WISELY

If using algorithmic trading software, ensure that your automated strategies are well-tested and aligned with your trading objectives. Automation can significantly improve trading efficiency but requires careful management.

Backtesting: Conduct thorough backtesting of trading algorithms to evaluate their performance under various market conditions. Backtesting provides insights into the strengths and weaknesses of your strategies and helps identify areas for improvement.

Optimization: Continuously optimize and refine your algorithms based on performance data and changing market dynamics. Optimization ensures that your strategies remain effective and relevant.

5. MANAGE DATA AND INFORMATION

Efficiently manage the data and information provided by trading tools to make informed decisions. Access to accurate and timely data is crucial for successful trading.

Data Analysis: Analyze historical data and trading patterns to identify trends and refine your trading strategies. Data analysis helps traders understand market behavior and develop effective trading plans.

Information Overload: Avoid information overload by focusing on relevant data and indicators that align with your trading approach. Prioritize the information that supports your trading objectives and filter out unnecessary data.

SELECTING THE RIGHT SOFTWARE AND TOOLS

When selecting trading software and tools, consider the following factors:

1. COMPATIBILITY AND INTEGRATION

Ensure that the software and tools you choose are compatible with your trading platform and other tools you use. Seamless integration is essential for efficient trading and analysis.

Platform Integration: Look for software that integrates seamlessly with your trading platform for smooth execution and data flow. Integration allows you to access all necessary tools and features from a single interface.

Cross-Device Access: Choose tools that offer access across multiple devices (desktop, mobile) for flexibility in trading and analysis. Cross-device compatibility ensures that you can monitor and manage your trades from anywhere.

2. COST AND VALUE

Evaluate the cost of trading software and tools in relation to the value they provide. Consider your budget and trading needs when making a decision.

Pricing Models: Compare pricing models (e.g., subscription fees, one-time purchases) and assess their suitability for your trading needs. Different pricing structures may offer different levels of access and features.

Features vs. Costs: Consider whether the features and capabilities offered justify the cost of the software or tools. Assess the value of the software in terms of its potential impact on your trading performance and profitability.

3. SUPPORT AND UPDATES

Check for the availability of customer support and regular updates for the software. Reliable support and regular updates are essential for maintaining the functionality and security of your trading tools.

Customer Support: Ensure that support services are available to assist with any issues or questions regarding the software. Good customer support can help resolve technical problems and provide guidance on using the software effectively.

Software Updates: Look for software that receives regular updates to improve functionality and address any security vulnerabilities. Regular updates ensure that your software remains up-to-date and effective.

Incorporating trading software and tools into your natural gas trading strategy can significantly enhance your trading experience and efficiency. By understanding the different types of software and tools available, and how to use them effectively, you can gain a competitive edge in the market.

Selecting the right software and tools involves careful consideration of compatibility, cost, features, and support. Conduct thorough research and evaluate your options to find the best fit for your trading needs and objectives. By integrating the right tools into your trading strategy, you can make informed decisions, manage risk effectively, and achieve your trading goals in the natural gas market.

CHAPTER 35: ACCESSING MARKET DATA AND ANALYSIS TOOLS

Access to accurate and timely market data is crucial for making informed trading decisions in the natural gas market. Market data and analysis tools provide the insights necessary to understand price movements, evaluate market conditions, and develop effective trading strategies. This chapter explores the different types of market data, sources for accessing this data, and the various analysis tools available to traders.

TYPES OF MARKET DATA

Market data encompasses a wide range of information that traders use to make decisions. Understanding the different types of market data will help you choose the right sources and tools for your trading needs.

1. PRICE DATA

Price data includes information about the current and historical prices of natural gas and related instruments. This data is essential for analyzing market trends and making trading decisions.

Real-Time Quotes: These are instantaneous updates on the bid (buy) and ask (sell) prices of natural gas and other financial instruments. Real-time quotes allow traders to monitor live market conditions and react quickly to price changes. The availability of real-time data helps traders capitalize on short-term price movements and execute trades at optimal prices.

Historical Data: This includes past price data, such as daily, weekly, or monthly prices. Historical data is used for trend analysis, technical analysis, and backtesting trading strategies. By studying historical price patterns, traders can identify recurring trends and develop strategies based on historical market behavior.

2. VOLUME DATA

Volume data indicates the amount of natural gas traded during a specific period. It helps traders understand market activity and liquidity.

Trade Volume: This metric shows the total number of contracts or units of natural gas traded over a given timeframe. High trading volumes often indicate strong market interest and can validate price movements. Conversely, low volumes may suggest a lack of interest or uncertainty in the market.

Open Interest: Open interest represents the total number of outstanding contracts that have not been settled or closed. It provides insights into market participation and the commitment of traders to their positions.

3. ORDER BOOK DATA

Order book data displays the list of buy and sell orders at different price levels, offering insights into market depth and liquidity.

Bid-Ask Spread: The bid-ask spread is the difference between the highest bid price (the price buyers are willing to pay) and the lowest ask price (the price sellers are willing to accept). A narrow spread generally indicates high liquidity and a competitive market, while a wide spread may suggest lower liquidity or higher market volatility.

Market Depth: Market depth provides a snapshot of pending buy and sell orders at various price levels. It helps traders gauge the supply and demand levels and anticipate potential price movements based on the order flow.

4. ECONOMIC AND FUNDAMENTAL DATA

Economic and fundamental data includes information about economic indicators, market events, and other factors that influence natural gas prices.

Economic Indicators: This data includes metrics such as GDP growth, inflation rates, employment figures, and interest rates. Economic indicators provide insights into the overall health of the economy and its impact on energy demand and supply.

Supply and Demand Reports: These reports provide information on natural gas production, consumption, inventory levels, and other supply-demand dynamics. Factors such as weather conditions, geopolitical events, and regulatory changes can significantly impact supply and demand.

SOURCES FOR ACCESSING MARKET DATA

To effectively access and utilize market data, consider the following sources:

1. FINANCIAL NEWS WEBSITES

Financial news websites offer up-to-date news, market analysis, and data related to natural gas and other commodities.

Examples: Bloomberg, Reuters, CNBC, The Wall Street Journal.

Features: These websites provide real-time news updates, market summaries, expert analysis, and access to economic indicators. They also offer opinion pieces, in-depth reports, and interviews with industry experts and analysts.

2. TRADING PLATFORMS

Many trading platforms provide integrated market data and analysis tools directly within their interface.

Examples: MetaTrader, TradingView, Thinkorswim, NinjaTrader.

Features: Trading platforms offer real-time quotes, charting tools, technical indicators, and customizable watchlists. They may also provide access to news feeds, economic calendars, and market sentiment indicators.

3. MARKET DATA PROVIDERS

Market data providers specialize in offering comprehensive and reliable market data for traders and investors.

Examples: ICE Data Services, S&P Global, Morningstar, Refinitiv.

Features: Market data providers offer extensive data coverage, including real-time quotes, historical data, and advanced analytics. They may also provide specialized data sets, such as weather forecasts and geopolitical analysis, that are relevant to natural gas trading.

4. ECONOMIC CALENDARS

Economic calendars track upcoming economic events and

data releases that can impact natural gas prices.

Examples: Investing.com Economic Calendar, Forex Factory Calendar, Trading Economics.

Features: Economic calendars list scheduled data releases, event impact ratings, and historical data. They may also provide alerts and notifications for important events and releases.

5. INDUSTRY REPORTS

Industry reports provide in-depth analysis and forecasts related to the natural gas market.

Examples: U.S. Energy Information Administration (EIA) reports, International Energy Agency (IEA) publications, OPEC reports.

Features: Industry reports include market forecasts, supply-demand analysis, and policy updates. They may also cover topics such as technological advancements, regulatory changes, and environmental considerations.

ANALYSIS TOOLS

Using analysis tools can enhance your understanding of market data and improve your trading decisions. Here are some key tools to consider:

1. TECHNICAL ANALYSIS TOOLS

Technical analysis tools help traders analyze price movements and identify trading opportunities based on historical price data.

Charting Software: Provides interactive charts with technical indicators, trendlines, and patterns. Charting software allows traders to visualize market data and apply various technical analysis techniques.

Indicators: Includes moving averages, Relative Strength Index (RSI), Bollinger Bands, MACD, and more. Indicators are mathematical calculations based on price and volume data that help traders assess market conditions and generate trading signals.

2. Fundamental Analysis Tools

Fundamental analysis tools focus on evaluating economic and financial factors that influence natural gas prices.

Economic Reports: Tools that analyze and interpret economic indicators and their impact on the market. Economic reports provide a detailed analysis of key economic data and its implications for the natural gas market.

Supply-Demand Models: Tools that forecast supply and demand trends based on industry reports and data. Supply-demand models provide a structured framework for analyzing market dynamics and identifying potential imbalances.

3. ALGORITHMIC AND QUANTITATIVE TOOLS

Algorithmic and quantitative tools use mathematical models and algorithms to analyze market data and execute trades. These tools are designed to enhance trading efficiency, improve decision-making, and automate complex strategies. Here are some of the key features and benefits of these tools:

Algorithmic Trading Systems

Algorithmic trading systems, also known as algo-trading or automated trading, involve using computer programs to execute trades automatically based on predefined criteria and market signals.

Predefined Rules: Traders can set specific rules for trade execution, such as entry and exit points, stop-loss levels, and profit targets. The software executes trades automatically when market conditions match the predefined criteria.

Backtesting Capabilities: Allows traders to test their trading strategies against historical data to evaluate their effectiveness. Backtesting helps identify potential flaws in the strategy and optimize it for better performance.

Real-Time Monitoring: The system continuously monitors the market and adjusts trading parameters based on changing conditions. It can execute trades within milliseconds, taking advantage of short-term price movements.

Risk Management: Includes features like position sizing, portfolio diversification, and automated stop-loss orders to manage risk and protect trading capital.

Quantitative Analysis Software

Quantitative analysis software provides statistical analysis and modeling capabilities for developing and backtesting trading strategies. These tools use mathematical and statistical methods to identify patterns and relationships in market data.

Data Analysis: Quantitative analysis software can analyze large datasets to identify trends, correlations, and anomalies. It uses techniques such as regression analysis, time-series analysis, and machine learning algorithms.

Strategy Development: Traders can use the software to develop and test trading strategies based on quantitative models. The software allows for the creation of custom indicators, risk models, and trading algorithms.

Optimization Tools: Includes features for optimizing trading strategies based on performance metrics such as return on investment (ROI), risk-adjusted returns, and drawdowns. Optimization helps fine-tune strategies for better results.

Real-Time Analytics: Provides real-time analytics and alerts, enabling traders to make informed decisions based on the latest market data and analysis.

Machine Learning and AI Tools

Machine learning and artificial intelligence (AI) tools are becoming increasingly popular in the field of algorithmic and quantitative trading. These tools leverage advanced algorithms and computational power to analyze complex market data and generate trading signals.

Predictive Modeling: Machine learning tools use historical data to build predictive models that forecast future price movements and market trends. These models can adapt to new data and improve over time.

Pattern Recognition: AI tools can identify complex patterns and relationships in market data that may not be apparent to human traders. They can detect anomalies, trends, and correlations in real time.

Automated Decision-Making: Machine learning algorithms can automate the decision-making process by generating trade signals and executing trades based on predefined rules and criteria.

Natural Language Processing (NLP): Some AI tools use NLP to analyze news articles, social media posts, and other text data to gauge market sentiment and anticipate potential market movements.

BEST PRACTICES FOR USING MARKET DATA AND ANALYSIS TOOLS

To maximize the effectiveness of market data and analysis tools, follow these best practices:

1. VERIFY DATA ACCURACY

Ensure that the data you use is accurate and up-to-date to make reliable trading decisions.

Cross-Check Sources: Verify data from multiple sources to ensure consistency and accuracy. This helps identify discrepancies and avoid potential errors in analysis and decision-making.

Real-Time Updates: Use sources that provide real-time or near-real-time data for timely decision-making. Accurate and timely data is essential for reacting to market changes and executing trades effectively.

2. COMBINE MULTIPLE TOOLS

Combine various tools and data sources to gain a comprehensive view of the market.

Integrate Analysis: Use technical, fundamental, and quantitative tools together for a well-rounded analysis. Combining different types of analysis provides a more complete understanding of market conditions and potential trading opportunities.

Holistic Approach: Consider both historical data and real-time information for a complete market perspective. A holistic approach helps traders identify long-term trends and short-term fluctuations, enhancing their ability to make informed trading decisions.

3. STAY INFORMED

Keep abreast of market developments, news, and economic events that may impact natural gas prices.

Regular Updates: Follow financial news, industry reports, and economic calendars regularly. Staying informed about market developments helps traders anticipate potential price movements and adjust their strategies accordingly.

Market Trends: Monitor long-term and short-term trends to adjust your trading strategies. Understanding market trends helps traders align their strategies with prevailing market conditions and identify potential turning points.

4. CONTINUOUSLY LEARN AND ADAPT

Stay updated on new tools, technologies, and methodologies to continuously improve your trading skills.

Education and Training: Engage in ongoing learning and training to stay proficient with new tools and techniques. Continuous learning helps traders stay ahead of market changes and improve their trading performance.

Adapt Strategies: Adjust your trading strategies based on new insights and evolving market conditions. Being flexible and adaptable is key to navigating the complexities of the natural gas market and achieving long-term trading success.

Accessing accurate market data and utilizing effective analysis tools are fundamental to successful natural gas trading. By understanding the different types of market data, selecting reliable sources, and leveraging various analysis tools, you can enhance your trading decisions and strategies.

CHAPTER 36: CHOOSING THE RIGHT BROKER

Selecting the right broker is a pivotal step in your journey as a natural gas trader. A broker acts as an intermediary between you and the market, facilitating your trades and providing access to trading platforms and resources. The choice of broker can significantly impact your trading experience and success. In this chapter, we will explore key factors to consider when choosing a broker, evaluate various broker features, and provide guidance on making an informed decision.

KEY FACTORS TO CONSIDER

When evaluating brokers, several critical factors should be considered to ensure you select one that aligns with your trading needs and goals.

1. REGULATION AND TRUSTWORTHINESS

The regulatory status of a broker is crucial for ensuring that your trading activities are conducted in a secure and compliant environment.

Regulatory Bodies: Check if the broker is regulated by reputable financial authorities such as the Commodity Futures Trading Commission (CFTC), Financial Conduct Authority (FCA), or European Securities and Markets Authority (ESMA). Regulation by such entities ensures that the broker adheres to stringent standards for financial reporting, capital adequacy, and operational transparency.

Reputation and History: Research the broker's reputation, history, and track record to assess its reliability and trustworthiness. Look for information about the broker's longevity in the industry, customer reviews, and any history of misconduct or regulatory violations. A broker with a solid reputation and a clean record provides a safer environment for your trading activities.

Customer Feedback and Reviews: Examine feedback from current and former clients to gauge the broker's reliability, customer service, and overall trading experience. Reviews can provide insights into the broker's strengths and weaknesses and help you identify any potential red flags.

2. TRADING COSTS AND FEES

Understanding the costs associated with trading is essential for managing your expenses and optimizing your profitability.

Commission Fees: Evaluate the commission structure, including per-trade or per-contract fees. Some brokers charge a flat fee per trade, while others may have a variable commission based on the size of the trade or the volume of contracts traded.

Spreads: Consider the spreads (the difference between the bid and ask prices) and how they impact your trading costs. Tighter spreads mean lower costs for entering and exiting positions, which can significantly affect your overall profitability.

Additional Fees: Check for other fees such as account maintenance fees, withdrawal fees, or inactivity fees. Some brokers may also charge for additional services, such as data feeds, research tools, or premium trading platforms.

Transparency: Ensure the broker provides clear and transparent information about all fees and charges. Hidden fees can erode your profits and create unexpected costs that can impact your trading budget.

3. TRADING PLATFORM AND TOOLS

The quality and features of the trading platform provided by the broker are crucial for executing trades effectively and analyzing the market.

Platform Features: Assess the platform's functionality, including charting tools, technical indicators, order types, and ease of use. A robust platform should offer a wide range of tools and features that support your trading strategy and enhance your market analysis.

Accessibility: Ensure the platform is accessible on multiple devices (desktop, mobile) and supports your trading preferences. A platform that offers cross-device compatibility allows you to manage your trades and monitor the market from anywhere at any time.

Customization: Look for platforms that allow customization of layouts, charts, and indicators. Being able to tailor the platform to your preferences and trading style can improve your trading experience and efficiency.

Reliability and Performance: Evaluate the platform's reliability, speed, and performance under different market conditions. A platform that is prone to crashes or lags during high market volatility can lead to missed opportunities and losses.

4. RANGE OF MARKETS AND INSTRUMENTS

A broker's range of available markets and trading instruments can impact your trading strategy and diversification opportunities.

Natural Gas Trading: Confirm that the broker offers access to natural gas futures, options, and other relevant instruments. The availability of a wide range of natural gas trading instruments allows you to implement various trading strategies and take advantage of different market conditions.

Other Markets: Evaluate the availability of other markets and asset classes that you may want to trade. Diversification across different markets and instruments can help spread risk and enhance your overall trading strategy.

Product Offerings: Consider the variety of trading instruments available, such as commodities, indices, forex, and equities. A broker with a diverse product offering can provide more opportunities for trading and investment.

5. CUSTOMER SUPPORT AND SERVICES

Reliable customer support is essential for addressing any issues or questions that may arise during trading.

Support Availability: Check the availability of customer support, including hours of operation and response times. A broker that offers 24/7 customer support can provide assistance whenever you need it, especially during critical trading periods.

Support Channels: Look for multiple support channels, such as phone, email, and live chat, to ensure you can reach the broker when needed. The availability of multiple channels allows you to choose the most convenient and effective method for communication.

Quality of Support: Assess the quality of customer support by testing their responsiveness, knowledge, and willingness to assist. A broker with a dedicated and knowledgeable support team can provide valuable assistance and guidance when you encounter issues or have questions.

6. EDUCATION AND RESEARCH RESOURCES

Educational resources and research tools provided by the broker can help you improve your trading skills and make informed decisions.

Educational Materials: Assess the availability of webinars, tutorials, and articles that can enhance your trading knowledge. A broker that offers comprehensive educational resources can help you stay informed about market developments and improve your trading strategies.

Research Tools: Look for access to market research, analysis reports, and trading signals that can support your trading strategy. Research tools can provide valuable insights into market trends, price movements, and potential trading opportunities.

Trading Community: Some brokers offer access to trading communities or forums where you can interact with other traders and share insights and experiences. Being part of a trading community can provide additional support and learning opportunities.

EVALUATING BROKER FEATURES

To make an informed decision, evaluate the following features offered by potential brokers:

1. ACCOUNT TYPES AND MINIMUM DEPOSITS

Different brokers offer various account types with varying minimum deposit requirements.

Account Types: Compare the features of different account types, such as standard, premium, or demo accounts. Some brokers may offer specialized accounts for specific types of trading, such as futures or options trading.

Minimum Deposits: Consider the minimum deposit requirements and ensure they align with your trading budget. A broker with a low minimum deposit requirement can be more accessible for new traders or those with limited capital.

Account Features: Evaluate the features and benefits of each account type, such as leverage options, access to premium tools, or dedicated account managers. Understanding the features of each account type can help you choose the one that best suits your trading needs and goals.

2. EXECUTION SPEED AND RELIABILITY

Execution speed and reliability are critical for ensuring that your trades are executed efficiently and without delays.

Order Execution: Assess the broker's order execution speed and whether they offer features like market orders, limit orders, and stop orders. Fast and reliable order execution is essential for taking advantage of market opportunities and minimizing slippage.

Platform Stability: Ensure the trading platform is stable and reliable to avoid disruptions during trading. A platform that experiences frequent downtime or technical issues can negatively impact your trading experience and performance.

Latency and Connectivity: Consider the latency and connectivity of the trading platform, especially if you are engaged in high-frequency or algorithmic trading. Low latency and stable connectivity are crucial for executing trades quickly and accurately.

3. MARGIN AND LEVERAGE

Margin and leverage options can impact your trading capacity and risk exposure.

Margin Requirements: Check the broker's margin requirements for trading natural gas and other instruments. Understanding the margin requirements can help you manage your risk and trading capital more effectively.

Leverage Options: Evaluate the leverage options offered and understand their implications for your trading strategy and risk management. While leverage can amplify your profits, it also increases your potential losses, so it's important to use it wisely and within your risk tolerance.

Risk Management Tools: Look for brokers that offer risk management tools, such as margin calls, stop-loss orders, and position size calculators. These tools can help you manage your leverage and protect your trading capital.

4. SECURITY AND DATA PROTECTION

Security measures are essential for protecting your account and personal information.

Encryption and Authentication: Ensure the broker uses encryption technology and secure authentication methods to safeguard your data. Look for brokers that implement advanced security measures, such as two-factor authentication and secure socket layer (SSL) encryption.

Data Protection: Verify the broker's data protection policies and procedures to prevent unauthorized access and breaches. A broker that prioritizes data protection can provide a safer trading environment and reduce the risk of cyberattacks.

Compliance with Regulations: Check if the broker complies with data protection regulations, such as the General Data Protection Regulation (GDPR) or other relevant laws. Compliance with these regulations demonstrates the broker's commitment to protecting your personal information and privacy.

MAKING AN INFORMED DECISION

To select the right broker for your natural gas trading needs, follow these steps:

1. CONDUCT RESEARCH

Conduct thorough research on potential brokers to gather information on their offerings and reputation.

Broker Reviews: Read reviews and ratings from other traders to gain insights into the broker's strengths and weaknesses. Reviews can provide valuable information about the broker's customer service, trading platform, fees, and overall trading experience. Consider both professional reviews from industry experts and personal testimonials from individual traders.

Comparison Charts: Create a comparison chart to evaluate brokers based on key factors such as regulation, fees, platform features, available trading instruments, customer support, and more. This visual aid can help you quickly compare brokers and identify the ones that best meet your criteria.

Forums and Communities: Participate in online trading forums and communities to gather opinions and experiences from other traders. These platforms can offer practical insights into how brokers operate, their reliability, and their customer service.

Regulatory Filings: Review the broker's regulatory filings and reports to understand their financial health and compliance history. This information can be found on the websites of regulatory bodies such as the CFTC, FCA, or ESMA.

Broker Websites: Visit the broker's official website to review their services, platforms, fees, and other relevant information. Pay attention to the transparency of their communication and how they present their services.

2. TEST WITH A DEMO ACCOUNT

Many brokers offer demo accounts that allow you to test their platforms and services without risking real money.

Demo Account: Open a demo account to experience the broker's platform, test trading features, and assess overall usability. This hands-on approach allows you to evaluate the broker's offerings in a real-world context without financial risk.

Evaluate Performance: Use the demo account to evaluate the broker's execution speed, platform stability, and support services. Pay attention to how the platform performs during different market conditions, especially during periods of high volatility.

Explore Features: Take the time to explore all the features and tools available on the platform. This includes charting tools, technical indicators, order types, and other functionalities that can enhance your trading experience.

Practice Strategies: Use the demo account to practice your trading strategies and assess how the platform supports your trading style. This can help you identify any potential issues or limitations with the broker's platform.

3. REVIEW TERMS AND CONDITIONS

Carefully review the broker's terms and conditions, including any agreements, disclosures, and policies.

Account Agreements: Understand the terms of the brokerage agreement, including trading rules, margin requirements, and fees. Pay close attention to any clauses related to dispute resolution, account termination, and data protection.

Disclosures: Review any disclosures related to risks, trading conditions, and potential conflicts of interest. This includes information about the broker's trading practices, order execution policies, and risk management procedures.

Fee Schedules: Examine the broker's fee schedules to understand all the costs associated with trading, including commissions, spreads, and additional fees. Make sure there are no hidden charges that could impact your trading profitability.

Leverage and Margin Policies: Review the broker's policies on leverage and margin, including any restrictions or limitations. Understanding these policies is crucial for managing your risk and trading capital effectively.

Privacy and Security Policies: Ensure the broker has robust privacy and security policies in place to protect your personal information and trading data. Look for details on data encryption, authentication methods, and data protection practices.

Choosing the right broker is a critical step in achieving success in natural gas trading. By considering factors such as regulation, trading costs, platform features, and customer support, you can select a broker that meets your trading needs and supports your goals.

PART 10: PRACTICAL CONSIDERATIONS

CHAPTER 37: SUCCESSFUL NATURAL GAS TRADES

Successful trading in the natural gas market requires a combination of knowledge, strategy, and discipline. This chapter will explore the key elements of successful natural gas trades, including the development of effective trading strategies, practical tips for execution, and examples of successful trades. By understanding these principles, you can enhance your trading skills and increase your chances of achieving profitable outcomes.

DEVELOPING AN EFFECTIVE TRADING STRATEGY

An effective trading strategy is essential for guiding your decisions and managing your trades. Here are key components to consider when developing your strategy:

1. DEFINE YOUR TRADING GOALS

Establish clear and realistic trading goals that align with your risk tolerance, trading style, and financial objectives.

Short-Term vs. Long-Term: Decide whether you are aiming for short-term gains or long-term investments. Your strategy should reflect these goals, with short-term strategies focusing on immediate market movements and long-term strategies capitalizing on broader trends.

Profit Targets: Set specific profit targets and performance metrics to evaluate the success of your trades. Determine what constitutes a successful trade for you, whether it's hitting a certain profit margin, achieving a set percentage return on investment, or maintaining a consistent win-loss ratio.

Risk Tolerance: Clearly define your risk tolerance. This includes the maximum percentage of your trading capital you are willing to risk on any single trade and your overall risk exposure.

Time Commitment: Assess how much time you can realistically commit to trading. This will help you choose the appropriate trading style and frequency of trades.

2. CHOOSE A TRADING STYLE

Select a trading style that suits your personality, schedule, and market outlook.

Day Trading: Involves executing multiple trades within a single day, aiming for small, quick profits. Day traders rely on intraday market movements and often use technical analysis and high-speed trading tools to capitalize on short-term volatility.

Swing Trading: Focuses on capturing short- to medium-term trends, holding positions for several days to weeks. Swing traders look for price swings and trend reversals, often using a combination of technical and fundamental analysis to make decisions.

Position Trading: Aims for long-term gains by holding positions for weeks to months, based on fundamental analysis. Position traders focus on macroeconomic trends and industry dynamics, allowing them to ride out short-term market fluctuations.

Scalping: A highly active trading style where traders aim to make small profits from minute price movements, often entering and exiting positions within seconds or minutes.

3. DEVELOP ENTRY AND EXIT RULES

Establish clear rules for entering and exiting trades based on technical and fundamental analysis.

Entry Criteria: Define the conditions under which you will enter a trade, such as specific technical indicators or market signals. Examples include a moving average crossover, a breakout from a chart pattern, or a significant change in supply-demand dynamics.

Exit Criteria: Determine when to exit a trade, including profit-taking points and stop-loss levels to manage risk. Set specific criteria such as a predetermined profit target, a trailing stop to lock in profits, or an exit signal from a technical indicator.

Flexibility and Adaptation: While it's important to have predefined rules, be prepared to adapt your strategy based on changing market conditions. Flexibility can help you avoid missed opportunities or excessive losses.

Backtesting and Optimization: Test your entry and exit rules using historical data to evaluate their effectiveness and make necessary adjustments. This process, known as backtesting, helps identify strengths and weaknesses in your strategy.

4. IMPLEMENT RISK MANAGEMENT

Effective risk management is crucial for protecting your capital and maintaining trading discipline.

Position Sizing: Calculate the appropriate position size based on your risk tolerance and account size. This ensures that you do not overexpose yourself to any single trade.

Stop-Loss Orders: Use stop-loss orders to limit potential losses and protect your trading capital. Set stop-loss levels based on technical analysis, such as below a support level or a specific percentage of your entry price.

Risk-Reward Ratio: Evaluate the potential reward relative to the risk of each trade to ensure favorable risk-reward ratios. Aim for a ratio of at least 2:1, meaning the potential profit is at least twice the potential loss.

Diversification: Diversify your trades across different instruments, markets, and timeframes to spread your risk and reduce the impact of adverse market movements on your overall portfolio.

Emotional Discipline: Maintain emotional discipline by sticking to your trading plan and avoiding impulsive decisions based on fear or greed.

PRACTICAL TIPS FOR EXECUTING TRADES

Executing trades efficiently and effectively is key to achieving successful outcomes. Consider the following tips:

1. USE TECHNICAL ANALYSIS

Leverage technical analysis tools to identify trading opportunities and make informed decisions.

Chart Patterns: Look for chart patterns such as head and shoulders, double tops/bottoms, and flags to signal potential price movements. Chart patterns provide visual cues about market sentiment and potential trend reversals.

Technical Indicators: Apply indicators like moving averages, RSI, MACD, Bollinger Bands, and Fibonacci retracements to analyze market trends and identify entry/exit points. Each indicator offers unique insights into market dynamics, helping traders make more precise decisions.

Volume Analysis: Consider trading volume alongside price movements to confirm the strength of a trend or a potential reversal. High trading volume often indicates strong market interest and increases the reliability of price signals.

Support and Resistance Levels: Identify key support and resistance levels on the chart to anticipate potential price reactions. These levels are critical for setting entry, exit, and stop-loss points.

2. MONITOR MARKET NEWS AND EVENTS

Stay informed about market news and events that can impact natural gas prices.

Economic Data: Track economic reports, such as inventory data, production levels, and weather forecasts, that influence supply and demand. Reports from the Energy Information Administration (EIA) and other industry sources are valuable for understanding market fundamentals.

Geopolitical Events: Be aware of geopolitical developments, such as conflicts, trade agreements, and regulatory changes, that can affect the natural gas market. These events can create volatility and influence long-term market trends.

Seasonal Trends: Consider seasonal factors that impact natural gas demand, such as winter heating demand and summer cooling demand. Understanding these trends can help you anticipate market movements.

Technological and Environmental Developments: Stay updated on technological advancements and environmental policies that may impact natural gas production and consumption.

3. EXECUTE TRADES WITH PRECISION

Ensure that trades are executed accurately and in a timely manner.

Order Types: Utilize different order types, such as market orders, limit orders, stop orders, and trailing stops, to manage trade execution. Each order type serves a specific purpose and can help you control your trades effectively.

Execution Speed: Monitor execution speed to minimize slippage and ensure that trades are filled at desired prices. Fast and reliable trade execution is essential for capturing market opportunities and managing risk.

Broker Platform: Familiarize yourself with your broker's trading platform and its features. This includes understanding how to place orders, set stop-losses, and monitor positions.

Trade Timing: Consider the timing of your trades in relation to market sessions, liquidity, and volatility. Trading during high liquidity periods, such as the overlap of major market sessions, can improve execution and reduce the risk of slippage.

4. KEEP DETAILED RECORDS

Maintain detailed records of your trades to track performance and learn from your experiences.

Trade Journal: Keep a trading journal to document trade details, including entry/exit points, reasons for trades, outcomes, and any observations about market conditions. This journal can be a valuable tool for reviewing your performance and identifying areas for improvement.

Performance Analysis: Regularly review your trade records to identify patterns, strengths, and areas for improvement. Analyze your win-loss ratio, average profit/loss per trade, and other metrics to evaluate your trading performance.

Lessons Learned: Reflect on both successful and unsuccessful trades to identify lessons learned and apply them to future trades. Continuous learning and adaptation are key to long-term trading success.

Goal Review: Periodically review your trading goals and progress to ensure you are on track to achieve your objectives. Adjust your goals and strategies as needed based on your performance and market conditions.

EXAMPLES OF SUCCESSFUL NATURAL GAS TRADES

To illustrate successful trading practices, let's explore a few examples of trades that demonstrate effective strategy implementation:

EXAMPLE 1: TREND FOLLOWING TRADE

Scenario: The price of natural gas has been trending upward, and technical indicators signal a continuation of the uptrend.

Entry Point: Buy natural gas futures when the price breaks above a key resistance level, confirmed by a moving average crossover.

Stop-Loss: Set a stop-loss order just below the recent support level to protect against potential reversals.

Profit Target: Establish a profit target based on the projected trend continuation and previous price peaks.

Outcome: The price continues to rise as anticipated, reaching the profit target, resulting in a successful trade with a favorable risk-reward ratio.

Key Takeaways: This trade illustrates the importance of identifying and capitalizing on trends, using technical indicators to confirm entry points, and setting appropriate stop-loss and profit targets.

EXAMPLE 2: SWING TRADING OPPORTUNITY

Scenario: Natural gas prices experience a temporary decline due to a short-term oversupply situation, creating a potential buying opportunity.

Entry Point: Buy natural gas when the price reaches a support level and shows signs of reversing, confirmed by a bullish reversal pattern. Look for bullish signals such as a double bottom pattern on the chart or a crossover of short-term moving averages above longer-term moving averages.

Stop-Loss: Place a stop-loss order below the identified support level to limit potential losses. Set the stop-loss a few cents or percentage points below the support level to protect against further declines while allowing some room for market volatility.

Profit Target: Establish a profit target based on the anticipated price rebound and previous resistance levels. Set the profit target near previous swing highs or known resistance levels where the price has struggled to break through in the past.

Outcome: The price rebounds as expected, reaching the profit target within a few days, yielding a profitable trade.

EXAMPLE 3: HEDGING STRATEGY

Scenario: A company involved in natural gas production wants to hedge against potential price declines.

Hedging Position: Sell natural gas futures contracts to lock in current prices and protect against future price drops. By selling futures, the company can ensure a predetermined selling price for its natural gas production.

Risk Management: Monitor the position and adjust as needed based on market conditions and price movements. The company may adjust the hedging position by buying or selling additional futures contracts to optimize the hedging strategy.

Exit Strategy: Close the futures position when the price moves favorably or as per the company's hedging objectives. The company can also roll over the futures contracts to extend the hedge if necessary.

Outcome: The hedging strategy effectively mitigates potential losses from price declines, helping the company manage risk.

Successful natural gas trades are the result of careful planning, effective strategy implementation, and disciplined execution. By developing a robust trading strategy, applying practical tips for execution, and learning from successful trade examples, you can enhance your trading skills and achieve favorable outcomes.

CHAPTER 38: ANALYZING MARKET TRENDS AND HISTORICAL DATA

Analyzing market trends and historical data is essential for understanding the natural gas market's behavior and making informed trading decisions. This chapter will guide you through the process of analyzing market trends, interpreting historical data, and using this information to forecast future price movements.

UNDERSTANDING MARKET TRENDS

Market trends reflect the general direction in which the price of natural gas is moving. Recognizing and understanding these trends is crucial for making strategic trading decisions.

1. TYPES OF MARKET TRENDS

Market trends are generally classified into three main categories:

Uptrend: An uptrend is characterized by rising prices, with higher highs and higher lows. Traders look for opportunities to buy during pullbacks within an uptrend, expecting the trend to continue.

Downtrend: A downtrend is characterized by falling prices, with lower highs and lower lows. Traders look for opportunities to sell or short during rallies within a downtrend, anticipating further price declines.

Sideways Trend: A sideways or range-bound trend occurs when prices move within a horizontal range, with no clear direction. Traders may use range-bound strategies to buy at support and sell at resistance, taking advantage of the price fluctuations within the range.

2. IDENTIFYING TRENDS

To identify trends, traders use various technical analysis tools and techniques:

Trend Lines: Draw trend lines on price charts to connect significant highs or lows, helping to visualize the direction of the trend. Trend lines can act as support or resistance levels, guiding traders in their entry and exit decisions.

Moving Averages: Use moving averages (e.g., simple moving average (SMA), exponential moving average (EMA)) to smooth out price data and identify the trend direction. Moving averages are commonly used to generate buy or sell signals based on crossovers or price interactions with the moving average line.

Trend Indicators: Apply indicators such as the Average Directional Index (ADX) and Moving Average Convergence Divergence (MACD) to gauge the strength and direction of the trend. The ADX measures the strength of a trend, while the MACD provides signals of potential trend reversals or continuations.

3. ANALYZING TREND REVERSALS

Trend reversals indicate a change in the direction of the market. Recognizing potential reversals can help traders adjust their strategies to capitalize on new market conditions.

Reversal Patterns: Look for reversal chart patterns such as head and shoulders, double tops/bottoms, and inverted head and shoulders. These patterns suggest a potential shift in market sentiment and can provide early warning signs of a trend change.

Divergence: Monitor for divergence between price and technical indicators (e.g., RSI, MACD) to signal potential trend changes. Divergence occurs when the price moves in one direction while the indicator moves in another, indicating a potential weakening of the current trend.

Candlestick Patterns: Pay attention to specific candlestick patterns that signal reversals, such as engulfing patterns, doji, and hammer or shooting star formations. These patterns can provide additional confirmation of a trend reversal.

UTILIZING HISTORICAL DATA

Historical data provides insights into past price movements and market behavior, helping traders make predictions about future trends.

1. IMPORTANCE OF HISTORICAL DATA

Historical data serves several important functions in the analysis of the natural gas market:

Trend Analysis: Historical data allows traders to analyze past trends and patterns, providing context for current market conditions. Understanding how the market has behaved in similar situations in the past can help traders anticipate future movements.

Volatility Assessment: Assess historical volatility to understand potential price fluctuations and adjust trading strategies accordingly. High volatility periods may require different trading approaches compared to low volatility periods.

Pattern Recognition: Identify recurring price patterns and anomalies that may repeat in the future. Recognizing these patterns can provide trading opportunities and help traders set realistic expectations for future price movements.

2. ANALYZING HISTORICAL DATA

Traders can use several methods to analyze historical data effectively:

Chart Analysis: Use historical price charts to identify trends, support and resistance levels, and price patterns. Charts can be customized with various technical indicators and drawing tools to enhance the analysis.

Statistical Analysis: Apply statistical methods to historical data to calculate metrics such as mean, standard deviation, and correlation. These metrics can help traders understand the distribution and relationships within the data, aiding in risk management and strategy development.

Backtesting: Test trading strategies against historical data to evaluate their performance and effectiveness. Backtesting allows traders to simulate trades using past market data to determine how a strategy would have performed under different market conditions.

INTEGRATING TRENDS AND HISTORICAL DATA INTO TRADING STRATEGIES

Combining trend analysis and historical data enhances your trading strategies by providing a more comprehensive understanding of market conditions.

1. DEVELOPING A TREND-BASED STRATEGY

Trend Following: Create strategies that capitalize on established trends by entering trades in the direction of the trend and using trend indicators for signals. This approach involves identifying strong trends and riding them for as long as possible, using trailing stop-loss orders to protect profits.

Trend Reversal: Develop strategies to trade potential trend reversals by identifying reversal patterns and divergence signals. Traders may use a combination of technical indicators and chart patterns to spot reversals early and enter trades at favorable prices.

Breakout Strategies: Implement strategies that focus on identifying and trading breakouts from established ranges or trendlines. Breakout traders aim to capture significant price movements that occur when the price breaks through key support or resistance levels.

2. USING HISTORICAL DATA FOR FORECASTING

Pattern Analysis: Use historical patterns and price movements to forecast potential future price action. By identifying similar patterns in the past, traders can make educated predictions about how the market might behave in similar circumstances.

Volatility Forecasting: Analyze historical volatility to estimate future price ranges and adjust position sizes accordingly. Traders can use volatility measures, such as the average true range (ATR), to set stop-loss levels and determine optimal trade sizes.

Economic Impact: Consider historical responses to economic events and news releases to anticipate potential market reactions. Understanding how the market has reacted to similar events in the past can help traders prepare for future developments.

3. RISK MANAGEMENT AND STRATEGY ADJUSTMENT

Adaptive Strategies: Adjust your trading strategies based on evolving trends and new historical data insights. Traders should be flexible and willing to modify their strategies as market conditions change, using historical data to inform their decisions.

Risk Management: Incorporate historical data into risk management practices by setting stop-loss levels and position sizes based on past volatility and price behavior. Effective risk management helps protect capital and ensure long-term trading success.

Scenario Analysis: Conduct scenario analysis using historical data to evaluate the potential outcomes of different trading strategies under various market conditions. This analysis can help traders identify the strengths and weaknesses of their strategies and make necessary adjustments.

Analyzing market trends and historical data is essential for making informed trading decisions in the natural gas market. By understanding and identifying trends, utilizing historical data, and integrating these insights into your trading strategies, you can enhance your ability to forecast price movements and achieve successful trading outcomes.

CHAPTER 39: COMMON PITFALLS AND HOW TO AVOID THEM

Trading natural gas, like any other financial market, comes with its own set of challenges and potential pitfalls. Recognizing and avoiding these common mistakes is crucial for maintaining profitability and managing risk effectively. This chapter will outline some of the most common pitfalls in natural gas trading and provide strategies to avoid them.

OVERTRADING

Overtrading is a common mistake that can severely impact a trader's performance and profitability.

1. UNDERSTANDING OVERTRADING

Overtrading occurs when traders execute too many trades in a short period, often driven by emotions or the desire to chase losses. This behavior can lead to increased transaction costs, reduced profit margins, and a higher likelihood of making errors.

Symptoms: Frequent trades with small profit margins, high transaction costs, and poor overall performance.

Causes: Emotional responses to market movements, lack of a clear strategy, or attempting to recover from losses quickly.

2. HOW TO AVOID OVERTRADING

To prevent overtrading, traders should focus on the following strategies:

Stick to Your Strategy: Follow a well-defined trading plan and avoid deviating from it based on short-term market fluctuations. Having a clear plan helps traders maintain discipline and avoid impulsive decisions.

Set Trade Limits: Establish limits on the number of trades per day or week to prevent excessive trading. These limits should align with the trader's strategy and risk tolerance.

Monitor Performance: Regularly review your trading performance to ensure you're meeting your goals and adhering to your plan. Tracking your performance can help identify patterns of overtrading and prompt necessary adjustments.

Avoid Emotional Trading: Recognize the signs of emotional trading, such as trading out of boredom or frustration, and take steps to mitigate them. Techniques like mindfulness, journaling, and stepping away from the screen can help maintain a clear head.

LACK OF RISK MANAGEMENT

Proper risk management is essential to protect your capital and prevent significant losses. A lack of risk management can lead to severe financial consequences.

1. UNDERSTANDING RISK MANAGEMENT

Risk management involves strategies and practices that help traders minimize potential losses and protect their trading capital.

Symptoms: Large losses relative to account size, frequent margin calls, and lack of capital preservation.

Causes: Inadequate stop-loss orders, over-leveraging, and poor position sizing.

2. HOW TO IMPLEMENT EFFECTIVE RISK MANAGEMENT

Effective risk management can be achieved through the following practices:

Use Stop-Loss Orders: Always set stop-loss orders to limit potential losses on each trade. A stop-loss order automatically closes a trade if the price reaches a specified level, helping to minimize losses.

Determine Position Size: Calculate position sizes based on your risk tolerance and account size, ensuring no single trade can cause substantial damage. A common rule of thumb is to risk no more than 1-2% of your trading capital on any single trade.

Diversify Trades: Avoid putting all your capital into a single trade or market to spread risk. Diversification can help reduce the impact of losses on your overall portfolio.

Regularly Review Risk Parameters: Periodically assess your risk management strategies to ensure they are aligned with your trading objectives and market conditions. Adjust your strategies as needed to maintain an appropriate level of risk.

IGNORING FUNDAMENTAL ANALYSIS

Fundamental analysis involves evaluating market conditions, supply and demand factors, and economic indicators to make informed trading decisions.

Ignoring fundamental analysis can lead to missed opportunities or losses, as traders may be unaware of the underlying factors driving market movements.

Symptoms: Trading based solely on technical signals without considering underlying market factors.

Causes: Lack of knowledge about fundamental factors or over-reliance on technical indicators.

How to Incorporate Fundamental Analysis

To effectively incorporate fundamental analysis into your trading strategy, consider the following:

Stay Informed: Follow news releases, economic reports, and industry updates that impact natural gas prices. Staying informed about market developments helps traders make better decisions and anticipate potential market movements.

Analyze Supply and Demand: Evaluate factors such as production levels, inventory data, and seasonal trends. Understanding the supply and demand dynamics of the natural gas market can provide valuable insights into future price movements.

Integrate with Technical Analysis: Use fundamental insights to complement technical analysis and improve decision-making. Combining both approaches can provide a more comprehensive view of the market and enhance trading strategies.

Assess Geopolitical Events: Monitor geopolitical events that may affect the natural gas market, such as changes in trade policies, sanctions, and international agreements. These events can have significant impacts on supply and demand dynamics.

CHASING LOSSES

Chasing losses occurs when traders attempt to recover from previous losses by taking excessive or high-risk trades.

Chasing losses can lead to further financial losses and increased emotional stress, as traders make impulsive decisions in an attempt to recover their losses.

Symptoms: Increased risk-taking, larger position sizes, and trading impulsively to recover losses.

Causes: Emotional responses to losing trades, lack of discipline, and unrealistic expectations.

How to Avoid Chasing Losses

To avoid chasing losses, traders should focus on the following strategies:

Accept Losses: Recognize that losses are a part of trading and avoid the urge to recover them immediately. Accepting losses as a natural part of trading can help maintain a balanced perspective and prevent impulsive decisions.

Stick to Your Plan: Adhere to your trading strategy and avoid making impulsive decisions. Following a well-defined plan can help maintain discipline and prevent emotional trading.

Take a Break: Step away from trading if you experience a series of losses to regain perspective and avoid emotional trading. Taking a break can help clear your mind and prevent further losses.

Set Realistic Goals: Set realistic trading goals and expectations to avoid putting undue pressure on yourself to recover losses quickly. Realistic goals can help maintain a balanced approach to trading and reduce the likelihood of chasing losses.

OVER-RELIANCE ON AUTOMATION

While automated trading systems and algorithms can enhance trading efficiency, over-reliance on them can lead to issues if not properly managed.

Understanding Automation in Trading

Automated trading systems can execute trades based on predefined rules and strategies, reducing the need for manual intervention. However, over-reliance on these systems can lead to potential pitfalls.

Symptoms: Overconfidence in automated systems, lack of manual oversight, and poor performance during market anomalies.

Causes: Blind trust in automation without understanding its limitations or maintaining regular monitoring.

How to Use Automation Effectively

To use automation effectively in your trading, consider the following:

Monitor Systems: Regularly review and monitor automated trading systems to ensure they are performing as expected. Monitoring can help identify issues early and prevent potential losses.

Understand Limitations: Be aware of the limitations and potential risks of automated systems, including their performance during volatile or unusual market conditions. Understanding these limitations can help you make informed decisions about when to rely on automation and when to intervene manually.

Combine with Manual Analysis: Use automation as a tool alongside manual analysis to make more informed decisions. Combining automated and manual approaches can provide a more comprehensive view of the market and enhance trading strategies.

Test and Update Systems: Regularly test and update your automated trading systems to ensure they remain effective and aligned with your trading goals. Testing can help identify potential issues and improve system performance.

NEGLECTING TRADING EDUCATION

Continuous education is vital for adapting to market changes and improving trading skills.

Understanding the Importance of Education

Neglecting trading education can lead to ineffective strategies, poor decision-making, and a lack of awareness of market developments.

Symptoms: Lack of knowledge about market developments, ineffective strategies, and poor decision-making.

Causes: Failure to stay updated on market trends, ignoring educational resources, and relying solely on past experiences.

Avoiding common pitfalls is essential for achieving success in natural gas trading. By understanding and addressing issues such as overtrading, lack of risk management, ignoring fundamental analysis, chasing losses, over-reliance on automation, and neglecting education, you can enhance your trading performance and protect your capital.

PART 11: CONCLUSION AND NEXT STEPS

CHAPTER 40: CONTINUED LEARNING RESOURCES

As the natural gas market evolves, staying informed and continuously educating yourself is essential for maintaining a competitive edge. This chapter provides a list of resources that can help you deepen your understanding of the natural gas market, stay updated on industry trends, and refine your trading skills. From books and online courses to industry reports and trading communities, these resources will support your ongoing learning journey.

RECOMMENDED BOOKS

Books provide valuable insights into the natural gas market and trading strategies. Here are some recommended reads:

The Handbook of Natural Gas Transmission and Processing by Saeid Mokhatab and William A. Poe: This comprehensive guide covers the technical aspects of natural gas transmission, processing, and distribution, providing a deep understanding of the industry.

Natural Gas Trading: From Natural Gas Stocks and Oil Companies to Oil ETFs and Oil Futures by Larry Williams: This book offers a detailed exploration of natural gas trading, covering strategies, risk management, and market analysis.

Energy Trading and Risk Management: A Practical Approach to Hedging, Trading, and Portfolio Diversification by Iris Marie Mack: This book provides a practical guide to energy trading, including natural gas, and discusses risk management techniques and portfolio diversification.

INDUSTRY PUBLICATIONS AND REPORTS

Industry publications and reports offer valuable insights into market trends and developments. Some key resources include:

EIA (U.S. Energy Information Administration) Reports: The EIA provides regular reports on natural gas supply, demand, prices, and inventories. These reports are essential for understanding market trends and making informed trading decisions.

IEA (International Energy Agency) Publications: The IEA publishes reports and analyses on global energy markets, including natural gas. These publications provide a broader perspective on market dynamics and trends.

Platts Gas Daily: Platts Gas Daily is a leading publication providing daily news, prices, and analysis of the natural gas market. It offers insights into market movements and price trends.

ONLINE COURSES

Online courses offer a flexible and convenient way to enhance your knowledge and skills. Here are some recommended courses:

Natural Gas Markets and Regulation by Coursera: This course covers the basics of natural gas markets, including pricing, regulation, and market dynamics. It's designed for traders, analysts, and energy professionals.

Energy Trading and Risk Management by Udemy: This course provides a comprehensive overview of energy trading, including natural gas. It covers trading strategies, risk management, and market analysis.

Technical Analysis for Natural Gas Trading by Investopedia Academy: This course focuses on technical analysis techniques for trading natural gas, including chart patterns, indicators, and trend analysis.

WEBINARS AND WORKSHOPS

Webinars and workshops provide opportunities to learn from industry experts and engage with other traders. Some platforms offering these events include:

ICE (Intercontinental Exchange) Webinars: ICE offers webinars and educational events on various topics related to natural gas trading, including market analysis, trading strategies, and risk management.

CME Group Webinars: CME Group provides webinars and workshops on trading futures and options, including natural gas contracts. These events offer insights into market trends and trading techniques.

Energy Risk University: Energy Risk University offers webinars and training sessions on energy trading, risk management, and market analysis. These events are designed for traders, analy and energy professionals.

ONLINE TRADING COMMUNITIES

Joining online trading communities can provide valuable support, insights, and networking opportunities. Here are some popular platforms:

TradingView: TradingView is a social network for traders and investors, offering real-time charts, technical analysis tools, and a community of traders to share ideas and insights.

Elite Trader: Elite Trader is a forum for professional traders, covering various topics related to trading, including natural gas. It offers a platform for discussions, idea sharing, and networking.

Reddit: r/NaturalGas: The r/NaturalGas subreddit is a community of traders and industry professionals discussing natural gas markets, trading strategies, and market news.

PROFESSIONAL ASSOCIATIONS AND NETWORKS

Joining professional associations and networks can provide access to resources, events, and industry insights. Some key organizations include:

AGA (American Gas Association): AGA represents the natural gas industry and provides resources, research, and networking opportunities for professionals in the field.

IPAA (Independent Petroleum Association of America): IPAA represents independent oil and natural gas producers, offering resources, advocacy, and networking opportunities for industry professionals.

NGSA (Natural Gas Supply Association): NGSA represents major natural gas producers and provides resources, research, and advocacy on issues affecting the natural gas market.

MARKET DATA AND ANALYSIS TOOLS

Access to reliable market data and analysis tools is essential for making informed trading decisions. Here are some recommended resources:

Bloomberg Terminal: Bloomberg Terminal provides comprehensive market data, news, and analysis tools for natural gas trading. It offers real-time data and insights into market trends and price movements.

Thomson Reuters Eikon: Eikon offers market data, news, and analysis tools for traders and analysts. It provides access to real-time data, charting tools, and market insights.

ICE Data Services: ICE Data Services offers a range of data and analytics tools for natural gas trading, including market data, pricing information, and risk management solutions.

Continued learning is essential for success in the natural gas market. By leveraging the resources provided in this chapter, you can deepen your understanding of the market, stay updated on industry trends, and refine your trading skills. Whether through books, online courses, webinars, or trading communities, these resources will support your ongoing learning journey and help you achieve your trading goals.

CHAPTER 41: FINAL TIPS FOR NEW TRADERS

As you embark on your journey in the natural gas market, it's important to remember that trading is a skill that develops over time. While the lessons and strategies in this book provide a solid foundation, your continued success will depend on your ability to adapt, learn, and refine your approach. This chapter offers final tips and advice to help you navigate the challenges and opportunities of natural gas trading with confidence.

START SMALL AND MANAGE EXPECTATIONS

Begin with Small Positions: Starting with small positions allows you to gain experience and learn from your trades without risking significant capital. This approach helps you build confidence and develop your trading skills gradually.

Tip: Use a demo or practice account to test your strategies and gain familiarity with the trading platform before trading with real money.

Set Realistic Goals: Setting realistic and achievable goals is crucial for maintaining a positive mindset and managing your expectations. Understand that trading success takes time and effort.

Tip: Focus on consistent progress and learning rather than aiming for unrealistic profits. Set achievable short-term and long-term goals that align with your risk tolerance and trading plan.

DEVELOP A ROUTINE AND STICK TO IT

Establish a Daily Trading Routine: Having a structured daily trading routine can help you stay focused and disciplined. Your routine should include market analysis, reviewing your trading plan, and monitoring open positions.

Tip: Dedicate specific times for market analysis, trading, and reviewing your performance. Consistency in your routine will help you develop good trading habits.

Regularly Review and Adjust Your Plan: Regularly reviewing and adjusting your trading plan is essential for staying aligned with your goals and adapting to changing market conditions.

Tip: Schedule regular reviews of your trading plan and strategies. Use these reviews to identify areas for improvement and make necessary adjustments.

FOCUS ON CONTINUOUS LEARNING AND IMPROVEMENT

Stay Informed and Educated: The natural gas market is dynamic and influenced by various factors. Staying informed and continuously educating yourself about market trends, economic indicators, and industry developments is crucial for success.

Tip: Follow industry news, subscribe to relevant publications, and participate in webinars and workshops to stay updated on market trends and developments.

Learn from Your Mistakes: Mistakes are inevitable in trading, but they provide valuable learning opportunities. Reflecting on your mistakes and understanding what went wrong can help you avoid repeating them in the future.

Tip: Keep a trading journal to document your trades, including the reasons behind your decisions and the outcomes. Use your journal to analyze your performance and identify patterns or areas for improvement.

MANAGE RISK AND PROTECT YOUR CAPITAL

Use Stop-Loss Orders and Position Sizing: Effective risk management is essential for protecting your capital and minimizing losses. Using stop-loss orders and appropriate position sizing can help you manage risk effectively.

Tip: Always set stop-loss orders for your trades to limit potential losses. Use position sizing techniques to ensure that no single trade can significantly impact your overall portfolio.

Avoid Overtrading and Emotional Decision-Making: Overtrading and making emotional decisions can lead to significant losses. Focus on quality over quantity and maintain emotional control in your trading decisions.

Tip: Stick to your trading plan and avoid making impulsive decisions based on fear or greed. Take breaks from trading if you find yourself becoming too emotionally involved.

BUILD A SUPPORT NETWORK AND SEEK MENTORSHIP

Connect with Other Traders: Connecting with other traders can provide valuable support, insights, and opportunities for collaboration. Engaging with a community of traders can help you learn from others' experiences and gain different perspectives.

Tip: Join online trading communities, forums, and social media groups to connect with other traders and share ideas and insights.

Seek Guidance from Experienced Mentors: Mentorship from experienced traders can provide guidance and support as you develop your trading skills. A mentor can help you navigate the challenges of trading and provide valuable feedback on your performance.

Tip: Look for mentorship opportunities through trading communities, professional associations, or industry events. A mentor can help you accelerate your learning and improve your trading skills.

MAINTAIN A POSITIVE MINDSET AND STAY RESILIENT

Cultivate a Growth Mindset: A growth mindset is crucial for success in trading. Embrace challenges as learning opportunities and focus on continuous improvement.

Tip: View setbacks and losses as part of the learning process. Stay motivated and committed to your trading goals, even during challenging times.

Practice Patience and Perseverance: Trading success takes time and effort. Practicing patience and perseverance is essential for overcoming obstacles and achieving your goals.

Tip: Stay patient and avoid rushing into trades. Focus on long-term progress and remain resilient in the face of setbacks.

As you begin your journey in natural gas trading, remember that success is a result of continuous learning, discipline, and effective risk management. By following the tips and advice outlined in this chapter, you can build a strong foundation for your trading career and increase your chances of success in the natural gas market.

Embrace the challenges and opportunities that come with trading, and stay committed to your goals. With dedication, perseverance, and a focus on continuous improvement, you can navigate the complexities of the natural gas market and achieve your trading objectives.

ABOUT THE AUTHOR

Usiere Uko

Usiere Uko is a Consultant, ILO Certified Trainer, and Business & Finance Author focused on financial independence and entrepreneurship. A former oil and gas engineer turned entrepreneur, he helps individuals and business owners build sustainable income, make smarter financial decisions, and grow resilient businesses.

He is a certified Business Development Service Provider (BDSP) and an ILO-certified trainer in SIYB and WIDB, and currently serves as Lead Consultant at Sageway Consulting and Training Coordinator at The Citadel Business Academy.

Usiere writes in a friendly and practical style, making complex financial and business ideas simple, clear, and actionable for everyday readers and entrepreneurs. He is based in Lagos, Nigeria.

BOOKS IN THIS SERIES
COMMODITIES TRADING FOR BEGINNERS

Gold Trading 101: The Beginner's Guide To Unlocking The Potential Of Precious Metals

Silver Trading 101: Smart Strategies For Silver Trading Beginners

Oil Trading 101: Understanding The Basics Of Trading The Oil Market, Cfds, Futures And Options

Natural Gas Trading 101: A Beginner's Guide To Profiting From The Energy Market

BOOKS BY THIS AUTHOR

Practical Steps To Financial Freedom And Independence: Money Management Skills For Beginners

Before You Trade Forex: Things You Need To Know If You Desire To Start Trading Forex Profitably

Before You Invest In Cryptocurrency: A Simple Guide To Understanding The Cryptocurrency Market

101 Common Money Mistakes To Avoid: And How To Fix Them. Book 1: Expenses. Money Management, Making Your Budget Work

How To Avoid Living Under Financial Pressure: A Simple Guide To Getting Back Control Of Your Finances

Financial Independence For Employees: Making

Your Job A Stepping Stone To Exiting The Rat Race And Living Your Dreams

Managing Your Money Post Covid: Financial Management Skills For An Era Of High Inflation And Market Disruption

Retire On Your Own Terms: A Simple Guide To Financially Literate Retirement Planning

Your Ultimate Money Makeover: Manage Your Money Better, Take Control Of Your Finances And Your Life

Teaching Kids Money 101: Simple Parenting Strategies For Raising Financially Literate Kids From Toddler To Teen Years And Beyond

Uncle Ben's Money Lessons: Book I: Do You Want To Work For Money? A Vacation Story With An Adventure Into The World Of Money

Nft Investing 101: A Beginner's Guide To Collectible Digital Assets

Stock Market Investing 101: A Practical

Beginners Guide To Online And Offline Stock Trading

Investing In Etfs 101: A Beginner's Guide For Building Wealth With Exchange-Traded Funds

Day Trading 101: A Complete Beginner's Guide To Trading The Markets

Forex Trading 101: A Beginner's Guide And Strategies To Profitable Currency Trading

Options Trading 101: A Beginner's Guide To Trading Stock Options

Futures Trading 101: A Step-By-Step Guide And Strategies For Beginner Traders

www.ingramcontent.com/pod-product-compliance
Lightning Source LLC
Chambersburg PA
CBHW071911210526
45479CB00002B/369